JOHN
LENNON

CAROLE
LYNN
CORBIN

JOHN LENNON

FRANKLIN WATTS
NEW YORK | LONDON | TORONTO | SYDNEY | 1982
AN IMPACT BIOGRAPHY

A GROLIER COMPANY

Photographs courtesy of
United Press International.

Library of Congress Cataloging in Publication Data

Corbin, Carole Lynn.
John Lennon.

(An impact biography)
Bibliography: p.
Includes index.
Summary: A biography of the rock musician
emphasizing his contributions to and influence on the
music and culture of the Sixties and Seventies.
1. Lennon, John, 1940-1980—Juvenile literature.
2. Singers—England—Biography—Juvenile literature.
[1. Lennon, John, 1940-   2. Musicians.
3. Rock music]   I. Title.
ML3930.L34C7   1982 784.5'4'00924 [B] [92] 82-11166
ISBN 0-531-04478-5

5

FOR
MY HUSBAND,
CHRIS

CONTENTS

THE END

1

In the fall of 1980, a friend of John Lennon commissioned artist Dorothy Spiegel to design life-size figures of John, his wife Yoko Ono, and their son, Sean. His friend knew this was the kind of wry humor John would appreciate, and he planned to give the Lennons the figures for Christmas. Ms. Spiegel made caricature faces on the dolls, exaggerating the noses: John's was thin; Yoko's wide. She dressed the figures in clothes that had belonged to the Lennons: the figure of John in a silk shirt and pants and round gold-rimmed glasses, the one of Yoko in a white suit, black silk blouse and sunglasses. Dorothy was preparing to start work on the figure of Sean when the project was abandoned. On December 8, 1980, John Lennon was fatally shot by a former fan.

An outstanding musician in his own right, John Lennon was best known as a member of the Beatles, the most widely loved rock group in the history of music. Of all the Beatles— John, Paul McCartney, Ringo Starr, George Harrison—John was the most idolized and had become a cult figure long before his death. For the past years, John and Yoko had lived in New York City in the Dakota, a stately apartment building on West Seventy-second Street.

On that fateful night in December, John and Yoko were returning from a recording session at the studio, the Hit Factory, where they had been working on a single from their new album *Double Fantasy*, their first record release in five years. After stepping out of their limousine, John and Yoko started to walk to the entrance of the Dakota, where a guard stood on duty. In the shadows of the building's huge archway stood Mark David Chapman. He called out, "Mr. Lennon." As John turned to face him, Chapman dropped into a combat position and fired his .38-caliber revolver at John, emptying five bullets into his shoulder and back. Yoko screamed as John staggered to the entrance of the Dakota. He fell face down on the floor of the entry office gasping, "I'm shot." Crying "help me," Yoko ran to him and cradled his head in her arms.

The police and ambulance arrived only minutes later. On the street Mark David Chapman calmly stood reading J. D. Salinger's novel *The Catcher in the Rye*. He was put under arrest as John was rushed to Roosevelt Hospital.

In the emergency room doctors made a determined effort to revive him, but they were unsuccessful. At 11:07 P.M., CBS News issued a bulletin about the shooting and minutes later confirmed Lennon's death. As the news spread throughout the city, people whose lives had been touched by John Lennon began to gather in front of the Dakota. When Yoko arrived home shortly after midnight she saw hundreds of saddened, stunned fans who had come to pay tribute to a man they loved, a man who had changed the world through his music. Yoko went up to her apartment on the seventh floor and placed three phone calls, one to John's Aunt Mimi, one to his son Julian, and one to Paul McCartney. Then she sent a message down to the fans: "John loved and prayed for the human race. Please do the same for him."

As the night wore on, almost all the fans quietly and slowly left. Huddled together against the cold night air, a small number of fans stayed on, playing "Imagine" over and over. The words of this song about a world without war, greed, or hunger expressed John Lennon's dream for humankind.

Across town, Mark David Chapman was in a room in the psychiatric ward of Bellevue Hospital. Only he knew the answer to the question, Why? He had been a devoted Beatle fan and he had liked the rebellious John the best. He strongly identified with John and imitated his activities. But Chapman had led a troubled life and had never found himself. On October 23, 1980 he signed out of work in Hawaii as "John Lennon" and never returned. He took John's words in the song "I Am the Walrus" literally: "as you are he/as you are me."

Earlier in the evening on December 8, as John and Yoko left the Dakota to go to the Hit Factory at about five o'clock, Chapman had asked John to autograph his copy of *Double Fantasy*, and John had scrawled his signature across the top of the LP. Then Chapman waited for John and Yoko to return home.

Messages of sympathy were sent to Yoko from all over the world. Tribute was paid to John by hundreds of musicians, critics, and world leaders. President Jimmy Carter said, "Lennon's spirit, the spirit of the Beatles—brash and earnest, ironic and idealistic all at once—became the spirit of a whole generation. He leaves an extraordinary and permanent legacy."

On the following day, December 9, thousands of fans crowded the streets around the Dakota to pray for John, to place flowers on the gate and to sing some of his songs such as "All You Need Is Love" and "She Loves You." They stood close together hour after hour as a freezing rain poured down. Yoko was secluded inside with several close friends, among them Ringo Starr and his wife-to-be, actress Barbara Bach. Outside the crowd waited for a statement from Yoko.

Raising their hands in the symbolic gesture of peace, John Lennon's fans gather on December 9, 1980, outside the Dakota apartment house where he was fatally wounded the night before.

Finally on December 10, she sent down a personal, heart-rending note, describing how she had told their son, Sean, about John's death:

> I told Sean what happened. I showed him the picture of his father on the cover of the paper and explained the situation. I took Sean to the spot where John lay after he was shot. Sean wanted to know why the person shot John if he liked John. I explained he was probably a confused person. Sean said we should find out if he was confused or if he really had meant to kill John. I said that was up to the court. He asked what court—a tennis court or a basketball court? That's how Sean used to talk with his father. They were buddies. John would have been proud of Sean if he had heard this. Sean cried later. He also said, "Now daddy is part of God. I guess when you die you become much more bigger because you're part of everything."
>
> I don't have much more to add to Sean's statement. The silent vigil will take place December 14th at 2 P.M. for ten minutes.
>
> Our thoughts will be with you.
>
> Love, Yoko and Sean

Yoko honored John's wish not to have a funeral service. His body was cremated and his ashes scattered at an undisclosed site in England. On December 14, in response to Yoko's request, 100,000 mourners came together in New York's Central Park for a ten-minute silent vigil.

Similar vigils were held in cities and towns around the world and especially in John Lennon's native Britain. Over 30,000 people gathered in Liverpool, the town where he was born, and at his home in Scotland, Paul McCartney said, "His death is a bitter, cruel blow. I really loved the guy." In their own ways thousands of others showed they loved John, too. A childlike sign written in crayon was placed in a candy store window in his old neighborhood. "We'll miss you, John," it read. His picture was put in windows, hung on walls, and taped to T-shirts and book bags.

John Lennon made a lasting impact on the world of music. He pushed the boundaries of rock music outward and gave it depth by incorporating classical, country, gospel and jazz elements in his songs. He experimented with electronically synthesized music and unusual sounds and instruments. He also left a legacy of unforgettable songs like "Imagine," "I Am the Walrus," and "Strawberry Fields Forever." His lyrics captured his time—the sixties—for he wrote honestly about love, suffering, loneliness, despair and hope and compassion. As one fan said, "The Beatles were always saying and singing the things I was feeling, the frustration and awareness. . . . It was like having an amplifier to my soul." Not long after John's death, rock star Bruce Springsteen opened a concert in Philadelphia with the words, "It's a hard night to come out and play; so much has been lost. . . . If it wasn't for John Lennon, we'd all be in a different place tonight."

It was not only on the music world that John Lennon left his mark. Courageous and caring, he spoke out against the Vietnam War and inequality, sometimes through symbolic gestures that were misunderstood or ridiculed. But he dared to be different.

"OUT OF THIS ROCK"

2

The Mersey River runs through Liverpool, a poor, rough city and the second largest port in England. During World War II Liverpool was a major naval shipyard and a prime target for Adolf Hitler's bombers. The planes of the German Luftwaffe flew overhead on October 9, 1940, dropping bombs on the city. It was the night John Winston Lennon was born. His mother gave him the middle name Winston in honor of England's prime minister, Winston Churchill.

John was the son of Alfred and Julia Lennon. Alfred, or Fred as he was known, was a handsome, fun-loving young man who worked as a ship's waiter; Julia was a slim, pretty, red-haired woman. She and Fred loved to laugh and sing and he taught her to play the banjo. Her sister Mimi said, "Julia was gay and witty. She never took life seriously." Despite her parents' objections, Julia impulsively married Fred on December 3, 1938 at the town hall. She came home, threw her marriage certificate on the table, and announced, "I've married him."

Julia and Fred got a small apartment, but during 1939 and 1940 Fred was working on a ship and was rarely home; he was out to sea when John was born. For the first eighteen months of John's life, Fred sent money to Julia, but then the money stopped. Julia was told Fred had deserted the ship, and for several months, she did not hear from him. When he finally returned home, Julia refused to see him, and Fred disappeared. At the height of John's success, Fred Lennon surfaced. John only saw him a few times, but he established a small pension for him.

Left on her own, Julia struggled to raise John. Her four sisters, especially Mimi, watched John and cared for him while she worked. When John was four years old, Julia moved in with a new man and Mimi offered to raise John. Julia accepted the offer.

John went to live with Mimi and her husband George. They had no children of their own and they owned a small house in Woolton, a villagelike suburb of Liverpool. Julia lived less than 10 miles (16 km) away, but John said he only saw her "sporadically." He felt abandoned and rejected and those feelings made him insecure and bitter. He hid his true feelings from Mimi and George.

As a small child, John had blond hair and looked a lot like Mimi, and she was pleased whenever he was mistaken for her son. She loved him deeply, yet she was very strict. She rarely bought him sweets or allowed him to go to the movies. She made him earn his allowance doing chores around the house. George was a softer touch, and John often turned to him for permission to go out or for money for candy. George became John's ally against Mimi and when Mimi sent John to bed without dinner, George would smuggle up some buns for him. George bought John a harmonica, which was his first introduction to making music. He played it for hours.

The first school John attended was Dovedale primary

school. At first he was an eager student and he learned how to read quickly. The headmaster described John as "sharp as a needle." He was already displaying an individualistic streak, however, and he hated to do routine schoolwork. He loved to read Richmal Crompton's *Just William* stories because he identified with mischievous William, who always saw events differently from everyone else. William required the members of his gang to have one adventure a week, "as dangerous as possible." John required the members of his gang to enact his favorite William tales. He often daydreamed he was Just William and wrote his own "William" stories.

John also wrote poems and stories for the school paper, the *Daily Howl*, and his own series of books. At the age of seven he wrote his first series, called "Sport and Speed Illustrated." They contained cartoons, and in imitation of the movie serials popular in the thirties and forties, they ended with the line, "If you liked this one, come again next week, it'll be even better."

Since he had a fanciful imagination, he loved the classic fantasy *Alice in Wonderland* by Lewis Carroll and he drew all the characters. Carroll's puns and word games appealed to John and as an adult the tale continued to inspire his creativity.

With each passing year, John showed less interest in school and more aggression toward other children. Despite Mimi's strict upbringing, he was constantly fighting. In fact, his closest friendship with a classmate, Pete Shotten, was cemented with a fist fight. When Pete called John "Winnie," John knocked him to the ground, sat on him, and ordered Pete to stop calling him "Winnie." As he got up and started to walk away, Pete jumped back up and again yelled, "Winnie!" John turned around in a rage. Suddenly his angry frown turned into a grin. John admired Pete's nerve and they went off to play together. They soon became the best of friends.

John and Pete loved to play practical jokes on their friends and teachers, and they quickly established a reputation as troublemakers. They were joined in their mischief by Nigel Whalley and Ivan Vaughan. According to Nigel, "John was always the leader. He was always the one to dare you. He never cared what he said or did." John often broke street lamps or played "chicken" with the buses. But it was always the other kids who were caught and Mimi was not aware of his reputation as the terror of the neighborhood. In spite of his penchant for trouble, John had a generous spirit. As a child, he willingly shared his candy or toys with his friends, and this generosity was a trait he always retained.

At the age of twelve, John entered Quarry Bank Grammar School where he rebelled against the regimentation of school by throwing erasers out of the window and playing hooky. He often disrupted the class by passing around his cartoons. His grades sank lower each year and in his third year he failed everything—even art. Although he was artistically talented, his assigned drawings were often sloppy or unfinished. He excelled only in drawing what he wanted, such as caricatures of the teachers. At the annual school festival John and Pete Shotten ran a booth where people threw darts at John's drawings of the teachers. Three darts cost twenty-five cents, and their booth always earned the most money even after the boys pocketed half the receipts for themselves.

Neither Mimi nor his teachers, according to John, understood his "genius," and they attempted to mold him into a "nice lower middle class English boy." But he was a rebel like his mother, Julia, and he described his childhood as "one long fight against the world." It became very difficult for Mimi to cope with John, especially after his uncle George died suddenly when John was fourteen. Without George to intervene between them, John and Mimi argued regularly.

John began to spend more time with his mother. As he had gotten older, Julia had visited him more often and they had grown close. John and Julia were very much alike; she not only encouraged his practical jokes, she played them herself. Unlike Mimi, she never lectured John about the importance of school or criticized his clothes.

At the age of fourteen, John was as unconventional as his mother, and to his aunt's dismay he dressed in the style of a "Ted" or "Teddy boy," the British version of the 1950s "greaser" look. John wore a leather jacket, tight black pants with stovepipe legs, and platform shoes. He brushed his long hair back on the sides and piled it high on top of his head in imitation of Elvis Presley, the king of rock 'n' roll. John idolized Elvis and particularly liked Elvis's songs "Heartbreak Hotel" and "Blue Suede Shoes." The rock 'n' roll sound from America was very much a part of the "Ted" style, and among John's favorite American pop stars were Little Richard, Bill Haley, Chuck Berry, and Buddy Holly and the Crickets.

John begged Mimi to buy him a guitar until she consented and bought the model he wanted: a steel-stringed Spanish one "guaranteed not to split." John never took lessons and he never learned how to read music. His mother taught him to play the banjo chords she had learned from Fred Lennon. But these used only four of the guitar strings and as a result, John was unable to play the bass strings on his first guitar. The first song he learned how to play was Buddy Holly's "That'll Be the Day."

In England in the mid-fifties a music fad called "skiffle" was very popular. It was a jazz style developed in the southern part of the United States and introduced into pop music by banjo player Lonnie Donegan, who recorded the first skiffle hit, "Rock Island Line." Skiffle was played on "instruments" such as tin cans, washboards, and kazoos—whatever was available. Since skiffle was easy to play, scores of teen-age skiffle bands sprang up and in 1956 John hastily organized his own group, which he called the Quarrymen, after the name of their school. His friend Pete Shotten played the washboard, and Nigel Whalley and Ivan Vaughan took turns on the tea-chest. Eric Griffiths played the guitar, Colin Hanton, drums, and Rod Davis, banjo. John, of course, was the lead guitar and the only member of the band with true musical talent.

After the formation of the band, John caused less trouble at school because he wanted to play at school events and dances. The motto of Quarry Bank Grammar School, which was located near limestone quarries, was a prophetic pun for John: "Out of this rock you will find truth."

The Quarrymen played at local dance clubs, parties and weddings, but they were rarely paid. Usually they received free Coke or meat pies in return for their performance. They played all the popular skiffle songs and at John's insistence, rock 'n' roll songs like "Blue Suede Shoes." He hated to memorize the words, though, and generally made up his own versions as he sang.

A major turning point occurred in John's life on June 15, 1956. That was the day Ivan Vaughan introduced him to four-teen-year-old Paul McCartney at a Woolton church social. Paul was as interested in rock as John and he impressed John when he wrote out the words of Eddie Cochran's song "Twenty Flight Rock" and sang some Little Richard songs, accompanying himself on the guitar. John admitted to himself that Paul was as good as he was. And Paul knew how to tune a guitar.

John faced a problem. On one hand, he wanted to ask Paul to join the Quarrymen because he was talented. On the other hand, he was not anxious to share the spotlight with him. A week later he decided to ask Paul to join the band. Soon afterwards, John smashed Pete's washboard over his head, a direct way of telling Pete what they both knew. Pete lacked musical talent and he, of course, quit the group.

After Pete left the band, he and John remained friends, but it was with Paul that John now spent most of his time. Paul taught John how to play guitar chords instead of banjo chords and he taught him how to tune his guitar. Paul was a better guitarist than John—and always was—but John remained the leader of the band through the sheer force of his personality.

John and Paul were opposites. Paul was conservative and eager to please; John, aggressive and rebellious. Paul avoided trouble; John looked for it and found it, often dragging Paul along. What bound John and Paul together was their mutual love of rock.

Of the two, Paul was the first one to start writing songs. When he sang his own song, "I Lost My Little Girl," to John in 1957, John was jealous and soon he began to write his own simple songs. From the outset, they were rivals, but they were also friends and they liked to collaborate in their writing. Sometimes they wrote entire songs "eyeball to eyeball," tossing lines back and forth. More often one of them wrote the major part of the song and the other suggested a line or two or the chorus. But regardless of who wrote what, they established the tradition of crediting all their songs Lennon/ McCartney.

John and Paul spent hours together rehearsing at Paul's house and John spent still more hours in his room composing and strumming his guitar. His schoolwork suffered and Mimi nagged him about wasting his time. Over and over again, she told him, "The guitar's all very well, John, but you'll never make a *living* of it."

THE BEATLES

3

John's school record at Quarry Bank Grammar School was awful and his teachers believed he was "hopeless" and "lazy." Only the headmaster, William Edward Pobjoy, thought John "might go far" because of his artistic talent. Pobjoy, prodded by Mimi, recommended John for the Art College of Liverpool, saying, "He had been a trouble spot for many years in discipline, but he has somewhat mended his ways."

Despite the lukewarm recommendation, John was accepted by the college. He enrolled in the fall of '57, and because he never showed up to select his courses, he was placed in the lettering department. John despised lettering and he was bored with the routine classwork. He upset many lectures and classes by passing around his drawings of hideous deformed children and all of his teachers disliked him except the unconventional Arthur Ballard.

Like John, Ballard hated the atmosphere of a classroom and he lectured at a tiny pub, Ye Cracke. Throughout the "lecture" John sat in silence, nursing his glass of beer, for he was generally too broke to afford more than one. Ballard said that at first John "struck me as the poor relation in the group." His work was either mediocre or unfinished. Then Ballard discovered a notebook filled with verses and caricatures that John had sketched. He thought they were extremely witty and he told John, "This is the kind of thing I want you to be doing." Ballard's encouragement, however, did not persuade John to attend clases regularly. He was far more interested in making music and spent his time rehearsing with the Quarrymen or performing at local dances.

The same year John started art college, Paul introduced him to George Harrison, who at fourteen years old was younger than either John or Paul. At first John paid very little attention to George, but George was an excellent guitarist and he taught John and Paul several new chords. George tagged along with the Quarrymen—who now consisted of John, Paul and Eric Griffiths on guitar, and drummer Colin Hanton—and occasionally John asked him to play with them. Eventually, John tacitly accepted George as a member of the band. Colin played with the band until the end of '58. He quit following an argument with John.

Mimi particularly disliked George, who dressed even more like a Teddy boy than John. She called him a "real whacker." John and Mimi argued more than ever over her criticism of his friends and his music, and he often left her house in a huff. John saw his mother frequently, and sometimes he moved in with Julia for days. He confided in her as if she were his sister instead of his mother.

The close relationship Julia and John had developed came to a tragic end when Julia was killed by a hit-and-run driver on July 15, 1958. At the time of the accident, John was at her house waiting for her to return from Mimi's. When the police told him what had happened he was devastated. He later confessed, "I lost her twice. Once as a five year old when I moved in with my auntie, once again when she died. It just absolutely made me *very*, very bitter." The hurt John felt caused him to develop a hard exterior, and he could only express his emotions through his music and his writing.

The emptiness in his life was partially filled by a classmate, Cynthia Powell, whom he started to date shortly after his mother died. John's interest in Cynthia surprised his friends because she was the complete opposite of him— quiet, shy and totally unlike his favorite movie star at the time, the sex symbol Brigitte Bardot. In an effort to please John as much as possible she made herself over—in Brigitte's image. She dyed her brown hair blond and bought tight pants and clinging sweaters. Cynthia was both attracted to John and frightened by him because he was very moody and violently jealous. He accused her of being unfaithful and of not loving him. Cynthia said, ". . . I was totally under his spell but I was really quite terrified of him for 75 percent of the time."

Yet Cynthia stuck with John. They went everywhere together, and she usually stood in the wings of the stage when he performed. She quickly learned about the top rock stars and songs. She even shared her allowance with John to keep him in guitar strings, for he was earning very little at the time.

John's only close friend at the art college was Stu Sutcliffe, a very talented painter whom John admired. Like John, he was individualistic and his huge paintings were unique; they bristled with excitement and brilliant color and they inspired John to paint. Stu also opened up the world of great art and paintings for John, and for a short time he took a renewed interest in his studies. Although he had failed his lettering exam and had been required to retake it, John was allowed to continue studying for his diploma, and Stu encouraged him to enter the painting department. He moved into Stu's combination studio-apartment and painted canvas after canvas.

John, in turn, opened up the world of pop music for Stu. Stu stood in the audience and tapped his foot when the Quarrymen played at school events. He longed to play with John's band and John encouraged him to play the bass guitar because he and Paul were then playing rhythm guitar, and George, lead guitar. When Stu sold a painting for £65 ($195) he used the entire amount to buy a bass guitar. John welcomed him into the group and taught Stu the basic chords. But Stu played poorly and Paul mocked him constantly. John sometimes teased him, too, but beneath his taunts was real affection and he was loyal to Stu. He turned down several jobs that were offered on the condition that he fire Stu.

John's band of four guitarists had been hindered by its lack of a drummer since Colin quit after an argument with John. Nevertheless, they managed to land a job as the regular band in the Casbah Coffee Club. It was a private club in the cellar of Mona Best's home. She served only coffee and soft drinks and charged one shilling (about twenty cents) admission. She paid John's band £3 ($9) per night to sing rock, rhythm and blues, and country and western songs.

Occasionally the group played at the Jacaranda, a squalid coffee house where Stu and John hung out between classes. They spent so much time at the "Jac" that the owner, Allan Williams, became their friend and manager of sorts. Through him, John found a drummer for the group, Tommy Moore.

Until this time, John's band had played under a variety of names. Now John hit on the name Beatles for the band. He liked the group Buddy Holly and the Crickets and in imitation of them he took the word beetles and changed it to *Beatles* as a takeoff on beat music. Williams, however, advised him to lengthen it as long names were in fashion. He suggested the name Long John and the Silver Beatles, but John compromised on The Silver Beatles.

It was Allan Williams who told John and Stu about an audition that London's top tour promoter, Larry Parnes, was planning to hold in Liverpool. He needed back-up groups to tour with the singers he managed and he wanted groups that were willing to work cheaply.

All the local bands auditioned. Dressed in suits, they all imitated the popular group Cliff Richards and the Shadows— all the groups except one: the Silver Beatles. Dressed in turtlenecks, tight pants, and sneakers, they were scruffy-looking and they played in their own loud style. Parnes liked them because they were different and he hired them to tour Scotland for two weeks with singer Johnny Gentle.

John was thrilled about the tour but as he set off, Mimi warned him, "The guitar's all very well, John, but you'll never make a *living* of it." This time she seemed right! John's earnings of around £18 ($54) per week barely covered his expenses. He survived on greasy fish cakes and French fries, traveled in a beat-up van, slept in run-down motels, and lived out of a suitcase—and he loved it! It was now obvious to John that he was going to make music, not art, his career.

His enthusiasm was somewhat dampened when the group returned to Liverpool. The Beatles'—they dropped "Silver" after the tour—only bookings were in rough clubs where gang fights and flying beer bottles were common. Fed up with the rowdiness of the audience and John's own rowdiness, Tommy Moore quit the band. Without a drummer the Beatles' future looked grim.

Then Lady Luck shone on them. Allan Williams was commissioned to book British rock groups for two nightclubs in Hamburg, Germany. He chose a popular local group, Derry and the Seniors, for the larger club, the Kaiserkeller, and because Williams owed the Beatles a favor for painting his own club, he booked them for the other, the Indra. The fee was £15 ($45) per week, and they had to find a drummer. Lady Luck continued to shine on the Beatles. Mona Best's son Pete, a handsome and sexy drummer, was free because his own group had just split up. He quickly agreed to join the Beatles.

Of the group, John was the most excited about the Hamburg engagement. It gave him a bright hope for the future, especially since there was no longer hope of him finishing art college. He was about to be thrown out.

He told his teacher Arthur Ballard, Mimi and all his friends that he was going to earn £100 ($300) per week! He exaggerated his fee by £85 ($255), but Mimi was not impressed. She had little hope for John when he told her that he was leaving college to play rock 'n' roll in a small nightclub in Hamburg.

"MAKE SHOW, BEATLES"

4

On August 2, 1960 the five Beatles—John Lennon, Paul McCartney, George Harrison, Stu Sutcliffe, and Pete Best— set off for Germany with Allan Williams, who had offered to drive them in his minibus. When they reached the ferry that would carry them across the English Channel to the Continent, the dock workers at first refused to load the minibus. They claimed it was too heavy, weighted down with the band's instruments, an amplifier and assorted pieces of luggage. They had also brought along a tin of homemade biscuits Mrs. Harrison had given them. But at the last minute John persuaded the captain to take them across the Channel. Once in Europe they made a madcap trip through Holland and Germany, arriving in Hamburg at night.

Like Liverpool, Hamburg is a vice-ridden port city. Prostitution is legal in one section of Hamburg, and it was in this infamous "red light" district that the Indra and the Kaiserkeller were located. The Beatles went straight to the Kaiserkeller to meet their employer, the owner of the two clubs, Bruno Koschmeider, a strange-looking dwarfish man. He so nearly resembled the caricatures John liked to draw that he left John speechless.

Koschmeider took them to see the Indra Club—a damp, shabby, gloomy place, but magnificent compared to the room he had provided for them at the rear of his movie house. The room was filthy and small—"like the black hole of Calcutta," Pete said—and the only bathroom was the theater's foul-smelling restroom. Yet, the Beatles were too inexperienced to complain, and they tolerated the awful conditions for seven weeks.

The Beatles played at the Indra from 7 P.M. to 3 A.M. with very short breaks. The audience was small at first, but as word of the band's performance spread, the audience grew larger. They sang rock 'n' roll songs like Little Richard's "Long Tall Sally" and "Good Golly Miss Molly," Chuck Berry's "Roll over Beethoven" and "Rock and Roll Music"—all of them John's favorite songs. The long hours, though exhausting, meant the Beatles were playing together more than they ever had before, and they were now growing together as a group and developing their own musical style.

Bruno Koschmeider generally sat in the audience shouting, "Make show, Beatles!" So they played very loud and emphasized the beat in a way that eventually evolved into their own unique style. They chug-a-lugged beer and John and Paul leaped around the stage. John in particular was delighted to act outrageous, once walking out onto the stage wearing a toilet seat around his neck. Though the audience of sailors was tougher than the Teds in the Liverpool clubs, John called them "Nazis" and yelled "Sieg Heil." They laughed. The rowdier he was the more the German sailors and greasers loved him. Soon the Indra was filled to capacity nightly and even rival groups, such as Derry and the Seniors, dropped in to see them.

After their performances, the Beatles usually went out to eat and at dawn staggered to their room and fell into a sound sleep on their squalid beds. Their alarm clock was the sound of gunfire blasting from the speakers in the movie theater, where gangster films and westerns were always playing.

John wrote to Cynthia every day. He sent her long letters filled with poems and declarations of his love for her. He also described the Beatles' living conditions, their performances, their escapades, and their two German friends Klaus Voormann and Astrid Kirschherr. He raved about Astrid's beauty, her unusual clothes, and her marvelous photography. Cynthia was filled with jealousy, but needlessly. It was not John Astrid fell in love with, but Stu. In his letters John enclosed dozens of photographs taken in photo booths in Woolworth's Five and Dime. He always posed in grotesque positions or made weird faces, much like his drawings.

During this first trip to Hamburg, John, Paul, and George became inseparable. They spent their afternoons roaming the streets of Hamburg or visiting the British Sailors' Society, a charity that provided cheap, hearty meals for British seamen in need of help. There the three musicians ate enormous amounts of eggs, French fries, and oatmeal. Sometimes Paul and John went off to write songs in a quiet room at the Society.

As the weeks passed, the Beatles' ear-splitting performances brought complaints from the Indra's neighbors and the police closed the club. But Koschmeider's contract with Derry and the Seniors was due to expire, so he moved the Beatles to the Kaiserkeller, where they were billed with Rory and the Hurricanes, a popular group also from Liverpool. The Beatles and Rory and the Hurricanes played alternately for eight or more hours every night. The two groups spent a lot of time together and John became very friendly with Rory's drummer, Ringo Starr.

After seventeen weeks, however, the Beatles' engagement in Hamburg ended unpleasantly. First George was deported because at seventeen he was too young to play legally in a nightclub. It is likely that Bruno reported him to the police when he became angry that the Beatles had played casually in a jam session at a rival club. A short time later, Pete and Paul were deported after they accidentally set fire to the old drapes in the movie theater. With the group scattered, John and Stu had no choice but to go home too. Astrid gave Stu the money for a plane ticket and John scraped up money for the train, although he hated traveling alone on the train for fear someone would steal his guitar. John arrived in Liverpool depressed and broke. He was so upset that he isolated himself in Mimi's house for two weeks before calling Paul.

The Beatles then went back to performing at dances and clubs like the Casbah, but the word quickly spread around Liverpool that their music had a "new sound." Because of their wild, foot-stomping performances in Hamburg, the Beatles' music was loud and pounding—totally different from the mellow music played by popular Cliff Richards and the Shadows, who often sang pop ballads.

The Beatles' "new sound" landed them a regular lunch-time engagement at the Cavern Club, located on a narrow street in Liverpool's fruit and vegetable market. The Cavern reeked of cabbage, cheese, beer, sweat, and dead rats, but it was a popular hangout.

Four times a week at the Cavern the Beatles played two forty-five-minute spots and, unlike most rock groups, they sang a wide variety of rock, country and western, and rhythm and blues songs, and they sometimes blended the styles. Disc jockey Bob Wooler says that they wanted to be different. "If everyone else was playing the A side of a record, they'd be playing the B side. If the others jumped around, they'd decide to stand still like zombies."

When John's Aunt Mimi and George's mother went to see them perform, Louise Harrison was full of enthusiasm. "Aren't they great?" she asked. But Mimi sourly disagreed. Now at age twenty-one, John was earning less than £5 ($15)

This early photograph of the Beatles was
probably taken around the summer of 1961,
when their popularity in Liverpool was
growing. Pete Best, the group's drummer
at the time, is shown here with (left to
right) John, George, and Paul.

a day, and Mimi still thought playing the guitar was no way to make a living.

Even if they weren't making money, the Beatles developed a large and loyal following at the Cavern. And they were conscious of cultivating a carefree image with the audience. As John explained, "None of us took any girls to the Cavern because we thought we would lose fans." In spite of this success, John grew restless. As soon as George turned eighteen years old, the Beatles obtained German work permits and returned to Hamburg.

They were booked for three months at the Top Ten Club, a larger and less rowdy club than the Kaiserkeller. There they played long hours, alternating with Tony Sheridan, a popular British singer who asked the Beatles to play the backup on a record he was making for the German company Polydor. The Beatles agreed to record the two songs, "My Bonnie Lies over the Ocean" and "When the Saints Go Marching In." The name "Beatles," however, did not appear on the label, because the German producer christened the group the Beat Brothers. It was nevertheless the first recording the Beatles made and an inauspicious start—or so it seemed.

Stu was not on the record as he had quit the Beatles several weeks earlier. He wanted to pursue his real talent, painting, and he had moved into a room on the top floor of Astrid's home where he was painting in a frenzy. But he and John remained close friends and John often went to visit Stu and see his work. When the Beatles returned home in July, 1961, Stu stayed in Germany to paint and to be with Astrid.

Back home in Liverpool, John moved in with Cynthia in a room she had rented when her mother moved to Canada. It was a cheap and rather dismal home, but they enjoyed many fun-filled moments there—especially when John had to avoid the landlady.

During the summer of '61 the Beatles were playing at the Cavern again and their popularity in Liverpool was growing.

They were voted the readers' favorite group in a poll conducted by the *Mersey Beat*, a guide to local clubs and bands for rock fans. John and Paul delighted in stuffing the ballot box, but the Beatles also received hundreds of real votes.

Mersey Beat was published by John's former classmate Bill Harry who devoted several columns to the Beatles and created a local demand for their record "My Bonnie Lies over the Ocean." For the first issue John wrote a humorous history of the Beatles, "Being a Short Diversion on the Dubious Origins of Beatles." He often contributed the spoofs on popular songs, short stories and captions, writing under a pen name, Beatcomber. He also wrote humorous personal ads: "HOT LIPS, missed you Friday—Red Nose." "RED NOSE, missed you Friday—Hot Lips." "Whistling Jock Lennon wishes to contact HOT NOSE."

John wrote long letters to Stu that were filled with jokes, verses and news about the Beatles. At first he was very enthusiastic about the Beatles' progress and their coverage in *Mersey Beat*, but by the fall he started to voice his disappointment about playing at the same clubs again and again. He was depressed and told Stu, "Something is going to happen, but where is it?"

In September John was so downhearted that he impulsively went to Paris with Paul to cheer himself up. "We got fed up," said John. "We did have bookings, but we just broke them and went off." George and Pete were naturally annoyed and the Beatles came close to breaking up.

BRIAN AND THE BEATLES

5

John's spirits were low in the fall of 1961. His goals were uncertain; he was going nowhere. Then Brian Epstein entered his life and changed it dramatically.

Brian was the son of Harry and "Queenie" Epstein, the wealthy owners of a furniture business in Liverpool. He was bright, but he never made good grades in the private schools he had attended. Like John, Brian "never quite fit in." He tried several careers, and having failed at all of them, he was totally at a loss when he went to work in his family's store as a salesman. To everyone's surprise, he was successful, and he particularly enjoyed working in the record department where he increased sales significantly.

As a result of Brian's success, the Epsteins opened two record shops, the North End Road Music Stores (NEMS), which Brian managed. He made a policy of filling all record requests, but he was perplexed one day when a customer asked for "My Bonnie Lies over the Ocean," by Tony Sheridan and the Beatles. Brian did not have the record in stock, and when he tried to order it, he was unable to track it down through his distributors.

Then Brian learned that the Beatles were playing at the Cavern, and on November 9, 1961, he went there to ask them about their record. Exceedingly neat and serious, Brian looked sharply out of place in the noisy young crowd at the Cavern and his appearance particularly contrasted with the sweat-soaked Beatles, dressed in tight black leather. He was dismayed by the Beatles' rowdy behavior; they smoked, drank and shouted while on the stage. At the same time, though, he found them "captivating" and he felt John gave off a magnetism. He wrote in his autobiography, *A Cellarful of Noise*, "I loved their ad libs and I was fascinated by this, to me, new music with its pounding bass beat and its vast engulfing sound." Until he heard the Beatles, Brian had liked mainly classical music and was unfamiliar with rock. Now he returned to the Cavern day after day to hear the Beatles. Soon he started to think about managing them.

In December Brian asked the group to meet him at his office for a chat. After they had talked a while, he blurted out his desire to manage them. There was silence. Brian's efficiency and his wealth impressed John and he answered in a low voice, "Yes. Manage us." Following John's lead, the others nodded yes. Another silence. "Where's the contract?" John asked, "I'll sign it." But Brian was so inexperienced that he hadn't thought to draw one up, and it was not until October, 1962 that they finally signed a legal contract.

As their manager, Brian's first goal was to establish a positive, professional image for the Beatles. Up and down the Mersey River the Beatles were infamous for their habit of lateness, and occasionally John or Paul never showed up at all for a performance. Now Brian personally picked up each of the four musicians and drove them to all their performances—on time. He also planned their performances with them, advising them to pay their best numbers instead of playing songs at random. He "strictly prohibited" smoking, munching sandwiches and guzzling drinks during performances, and also made them stop shouting and swearing at the audience.

Brian insisted that their personal appearance project a clean-cut image. He prodded them to wash themselves and their hair more often, and he even selected new suits with velvet collars and thin lapels for them—suits similar to the ones worn by Cliff Richards's group, the Shadows. Some months before, in his article "Being a Short Diversion on the Dubious Origins of Beatles," in *Mersey Beat*, John had written, "So suddenly all back in Liverpool Village were many groups playing in grey suits and Jim said, 'Why have you no grey suits?' 'We don't like, them, Jim' we said, speaking to Jim." Faced with wearing a "grey suit" of his own, John argued with Brian. But Paul and the others sided with Brian, and John uncharacteristically gave in. Occasionally he launched minor rebellions and wore his tie undone, but Brian always straightened it before he went on stage.

Brian had a difficult job keeping John in check. The two fought often; yet, of the four Beatles, John formed the closest friendship with Brian. And John respected him as a manager. "We'd never have made it without him," John said. "In the early days, Brian contributed as much as we did." Like all of John's friends, however, Brian was subjected to his cutting humor and sarcasm. Once when he criticized the group's singing, John snapped in a nasty tone, "You stick to the percentages and we'll look after the music."

Brian arranged many bookings for the Beatles, but his real goal was to land a recording contract for them. As a successful record seller, Brian had contacts in the industry and he used his influence to obtain an audition at Decca, a major record company. After hearing the Beatles perform at the Cavern, Decca's Mike Smith, assistant in the Artist and

Repertoire (A&R) Department, set up a formal studio audition for them in London on January 1, 1962.

New Year's Eve was cold and snowy when the Beatles set off in their van for London. The next morning four nervous young men arrived at the studio for their first audition. Urged by Brian to demonstrate their unusual arrangements of standards, they sang several popular songs like "Red Sails in the Sunset," "The Sheik of Araby," and "Your Feet's Too Big." John insisted that they also sing three Lennon/McCartney originals: "Hello Little Girl," "Love of the Loved," and "Like Dreamers Do."

The Beatles were all worried, including their usually arrogant leader John, and as a result, their performance lacked the sparkle of their live shows. Paul's voice even cracked. Nevertheless, Mike insisted that he liked the tapes, and they left the studio in high spirits. They were sure they would be offered a contract, and Brian took them out to dinner to celebrate.

Weeks went by before the Beatles heard from Decca. Finally, after three months, the company turned them down. With soloists like Ray Charles topping the sales charts, Decca's executives told Brian, "Groups of guitars are on their way out." But Brian angrily retorted, "One day the Beatles will be bigger than Elvis." Like the others, John was disappointed not to have gotten the contract, but he said optimistically that they'd simply have to sign with another company. In his letters to Stu Sutcliffe, John expressed feelings of self-doubt and disillusionment, yet he showed only confidence to Paul, George, and Pete. He was their "cheerleader." Whenever they were down, he'd shout, "Where are we going, fellas?"

"To the top," they all would cry.

"What top?"

"To the Toppermost of the Poppermost, Johnny."

While Brian began to make his rounds of the record companies with a "demo" tape, the Beatles returned to Hamburg for the third time. John looked forward to seeing his friend Stu again, but when he arrived in Hamburg he was stunned by the news that Stu had died of a brain tumor that same day. John had lost his best friend and confidant, yet he hid his emotions just as he had done when his uncle and his mother had died. John's sorrow was reflected only in a small gesture—in asking Mrs. Sutcliffe if he might have Stu's scarf.

The Star Club, where the Beatles were booked, was the biggest and newest club in Hamburg, but the audiences of French, American, and British sailors and local German hoodlums were as tough as those at the Kaiserkeller. In Brian's absence, John reverted to his rowdy ways both on stage and off.

Meanwhile, at home one record company after another had rejected the Beatles. Brian's hopes were falling when he played the demo for the head of A&R at Parlophone Records, George Martin. Parlophone was a subsidiary of EMI, the largest record company in the world at the time. Although his label was known primarily for its comedy records, Martin was interested in signing a rock group to increase sales. He listened to the demo attentively and what he heard made him agree to give the Beatles a studio audition. He later said he liked their "unusual quality—a certain roughness."

His hopes and spirit renewed, Brian sent the Beatles a telegram: CONGRATULATIONS BOYS, EMI REQUESTS RECORDING SESSION. PLEASE REHEARSE NEW MATERIAL. John and Paul sat down at once and wrote postcards to Brian. "Please wire £10,000 ($30,000) advance royalties," wrote Paul, and John asked, "When are we going to be millionaires?"

When the Beatles returned from Hamburg at the beginning of the summer, they auditioned for George Martin, singing a number of their own songs such as "Love Me Do," as well as some standards. He liked them, but not enough to commit himself immediately. He told Brian privately, "The drumming isn't at all what I want. If we do make a record, I'd prefer to use my own drummer.''

In fact, Pete had never fit into the group. In contrast to the others he was too serious, even sullen. When Brian repeated Martin's comment about Pete to John, Paul, and George, they decided to fire him and hire Ringo Starr as their drummer. The Beatles had met Ringo in Hamburg when he was the drummer for Rory and the Hurricanes, and they liked his keen sense of humor and style of drumming. John had spent hours hanging around Hamburg with Ringo, who wore a beard in those days, and it was John who called him with the news. "You're in," he told Ringo, adding, "The beard will have to go." John also told him that he'd have to wear his hair in bangs, known variously as the "French style" and the "Julius Caesar."

The origin of the hair style the Beatles made famous is buried in legend. Supposedly, Astrid had cut Stu's hair into bangs in 1960 and George had imitated it. John and Paul copied it too, but then had returned to their "Elvis" style. They had not worn bangs again, some say, until they had it cut on their Paris escapade in the fall of 1961. One thing is certain. By the end of 1962, the four Beatles—John, Paul, George, and Ringo—all sported the same bang-style hairdo. They looked like four peas in a pod.

Ringo was the Beatles' drummer when George Martin finally called them and offered them a recording contract— but no one had told Martin. When the Beatles arrived at the studio to cut their first record, "Love Me Do," they found out that Martin had hired a drummer for the session. Ringo was reduced to playing the tambourine, and he looked so forlorn that Martin recorded a take with him on the drums. It was the take he used for the record "Love Me Do." On the B side, "P.S. I Love You," Ringo only played maracas. Both sides of the Beatles' first single were Lennon/McCartney originals, an unusual occurrence in the music business then, when unknown groups generally recorded songs by well-known writers. But Martin had liked their simple catchy songs and he had especially liked John's harmonica passage on "Love Me Do." Since he frankly had not known what to have the Beatles record, he used the two originals. Before the session he had even toyed with the idea of just using the Beatles as a backup group or of making either John or Paul the lead singer. In the end, however, he had decided not to tamper with the group because their voices were balanced. Paul sang high tenor, sometimes falsetto, John, high baritone. George sang harmony, and Ringo sang in a low, sometimes off-key, voice.

Brian and the Beatles desperately wanted "Love Me Do" to make the top 20, the mark of success for a record and a sure-fire way to get air time on the radio. According to legend, Brian took no chances. He bought 10,000 copies of "Love Me Do" himself. Slowly the song moved up the charts to reach the number 17 spot. It was a large accomplishment for a new group singing a new song.

The summer of 1962 was an eventful time for John. Not only did he make his first recording, but he and Cynthia were married on August 23rd, a few weeks after her doctor had confirmed that she was pregnant. When she broke the news to John, he was silent for a few minutes and then blurted out, "There's only one thing for it, Cyn, we'll have to get married." Neither Cynthia's mother nor John's aunt Mimi attended the wedding. Her mother was in Canada, and Mimi refused to come because Cynthia was pregnant.

The wedding ceremony took place in a registry office in Liverpool with a pneumatic drill outside drowning out their vows. Cynthia wore a purple and black suit with a white frilly blouse—hand-me-downs from Astrid. John dressed in a black suit as did Paul and George. Brian was the best man and he treated them all to a chicken dinner after the ceremony. John and Cynthia kept their marriage a secret from the local press. John was afraid he'd lose fans; Cynthia was afraid she'd be confronted by them.

As a wedding gift, Brian gave the couple the use of a furnished apartment that he rented but rarely used. Although it was elegant compared to Cynthia's boarding house room, it was in a tough neighborhood near the Liverpool Art College. Since John was either touring, working, or rehearsing most of the time, Cynthia found herself alone and scared in the unsavory area. She quickly accepted Mimi's offer to use the second floor of her house as an apartment. It was Mimi's way to apologize for her absence at their wedding, but she was still skeptical that John could make a living as a musician. It would only be a matter of months, however, before John and Cynthia could afford an apartment of their own in London, for John's career was about to take off.

BEATLEMANIA
6

Less than three months after recording "Love Me Do" the Beatles made their second single, "Please Please Me," a song that John both wrote and sang himself. In a manner George Martin later described as "self-opinionated" and "very sure" of himself, John insisted on using it instead of the song that Martin had selected.

The sheet music of "Please Please Me" was published by George Martin's friend, Dick James. With Martin's encouragement, James set up a company called Northern Songs to publish the Lennon/McCartney songs, but the composers had to give up the ownership of the copyrights to Northern Songs. It was a standard deal in the music business, but John later resented having to ask Northern Songs for permission to record his own compositions. He said it "used to make me suffer, and think I'd been robbed and ripped off."

Dick James, however, did more than just publish the Beatles' songs. He had a hand in establishing the group when he arranged for them to appear on the TV variety show "Thank Your Lucky Stars" the day "Please Please Me" was released—January 12, 1963. It was their first appearance on national television in England, and the audience was packed with fans from Liverpool who shrieked and screamed as they sang. The national exposure promoted sales of "Please Please Me," and seven weeks later it reached number one on the record chart.

Eager to capitalize on the success of "Please Please Me," Martin rushed out an album of the same title. This album, the Beatles' first, was made in approximately thirteen hours and cost only £400 ($1200). It included rock classics like "Twist and Shout," which John literally shouted and Lennon/McCartney songs like "Do You Want to Know a Secret?" and "I Saw Her Standing There." The number of originals surprised music critics as it was very unusual at the time for rock stars to write their own music. This feature set the Beatles apart from other performers. Soon the critics started talking about a "Mersey" sound and record companies sent representatives to Liverpool to sign up local groups such as Gerry and the Pacemakers.

Paul and John, however, often denied that a "Mersey" sound existed. In fact, "Please Please Me" imitated an American phenomenon, the "Motown sound." Developed by the American record producer Phil Spector for Motown Records, the style was popularized by groups and performers such as Smokey Robinson and the Miracles, the Temptations, Diana Ross and the Supremes, and Stevie Wonder. To achieve the "Motown sound," also known as the "wall of sound" technique, the tracks are mixed in a way that makes the instruments indistinguishable, and produces a sound that envelops the listener.

In their early years the Beatles freely adapted techniques from other groups though they never merely copied. They always added their own touches. John said their first gimmick was the harmonica riff, which they used in "Love Me Do," "Please Please Me" and other songs.

"Please Please Me" topped the LP charts in Britain for 30 weeks and established the Beatles as hot new rock stars. They found themselves whizzing from town to town for one-night shows and TV appearances. John was even on the road when Cynthia gave birth to their son, named John Charles Julian in honor of John, Cynthia's father, and John's mother, Julia. John called him Julian and saw him for the first time when he was seven days old. To avoid his fans, John tried to disguise himself before going to the hospital, but already he was drawing crowds wherever he went. Bubbling over with excitement, John peeked through the nursery window to see his son as nurses and patients gathered in the hospital corridor to see John! Cynthia was "unnerved" when she realized that they were going to have to live like goldfish. And it was just the beginning.

The Beatles were on their way to recording a phenomenal number of consecutive hits, which established the distinctive features of their music. Their third single, "From Me to You," was a Lennon/McCartney original similar to "Please Please Me." Paul sang it in a falsetto style popular in the early sixties. The "woo, woo" phrase which linked the chorus and the verse was taken from the Isley Brothers' song "Twist and Shout," but John and Paul went on to use it in so many songs that it soon became a Beatle trademark like the cheerful "yeah, yeah, yeah" chorus of their next song, "She Loves You."

Most of the early Lennon/McCartney hits were true collaborations, written as the Beatles traveled or as they whiled away the hours in hotel rooms. Paul gave their songs a light, optimistic touch while John contributed their cutting edge and "bluesy" moods. Their contrasting styles balanced the music and the lyrics and made them unique.

The Beatles' string of hits made them superstars, and they were courted by the press for interviews, which they willingly gave. John dominated the interviews with his witty one-liners and the press quickly labeled him the "wit," "rebel," and "intellectual" of the group. The dark, cruel side of John's humor was hidden from the press, in part, because Brian "muzzled" John, and in part, because John took delight in putting the press on. He turned press conferences into a game in order to keep from exploding when he was asked repetitious questions. The picture the press painted of John as a witty, cheerful boy was very deceiving. He was still aggressive, moody, rowdy, and insecure.

The Beatles' story was told and retold because it contained a theme everyone loved: Poor boy makes good. Here were four poor boys who made good, so the story was four times as good! Ringo was from a lower class family, but the others were from lower middle and middle class families. Nevertheless, the legend developed that they all grew up in the slums.

Soon each of the Beatles was known by name and by personality traits. The fact that they were known as individuals was unusual for a group and added to their popularity for they each attracted their own personal fans. Paul was popular with the young girls because he was handsome and baby-faced, Ringo was popular for the opposite reason—he was homely. George was the most reserved and had the fewest fans, whereas John attracted the most devoted fans because they identified with his rebellious spirit.

For young people, the Beatles' mop-like hair became a special symbol of rebellion, and the kids loved their flip answers about it. Reporters often asked, "Do you wear wigs?" to which John usually answered, "If they are, they must be the only wigs with dandruff." And when asked the name of their hairstyle Ringo replied simply, "Arthur." It wasn't long, though, before adults as well as teen-agers accepted the Beatles, realizing that their well-scrubbed image contrasted with the tough rockers like Elvis and his imitators.

The Beatles were even honored with an invitation to perform at the Royal Command Variety Performance at Buckingham Palace in November in 1963. John was reluctant to do it, but Brian insisted that it would be good for their image. For the first and last time, they accepted.

The Beatles sang several songs and cracked jokes, and for the last song, "Twist and Shout," John asked the audience to join in. "Will the people in the cheap seats clap your hands?" he asked. "All the rest of you, if you'll just rattle your jewelry." John was mocking the class consciousness of British society in front of an audience of royalty and wealthy lords and ladies. Brian sighed; it was typical of John to make an inflammatory statement. But the audience laughed.

The next day a front page report in the newspaper the *Daily Mirror* about their performance for the Royal Family bore the headline:

BEATLEMANIA!

Beatlemania spread throughout Great Britain faster than the black plague during the Middle Ages, but the Beatles' enormous success in Great Britain in 1963 was not matched in the United States. In fact, their name was barely known in the music field. The "California sound," with such songs as the Beach Boys "Surfin' U.S.A.," was the "in" music in the pop field. As a result, Capitol Records, the U.S. affiliate of EMI, had not felt the Beatles could succeed and had refused to release the Beatles' singles. "Please Please Me" and "From Me to You" had been released in the United States by the small company Vee Jay, but the sales had been poor. They never even made the charts. Capitol even refused to release "She Loves You" when it topped the British charts for eight weeks. Released in the United States by Swan, "She Loves You" never even made the top 100.

With the hope of winning the American public, Brian Epstein went to the United States in November 1963 for two purposes: to persuade Capitol to release the Beatles' newest

John continues his performance while a victim of "Beatlemania" is carried off the stage during a show in Manchester, England, in 1963.

single, "I Want to Hold Your Hand," and to sign a contract for the Beatles to perform on the TV variety program, "The Ed Sullivan Show." Ed Sullivan was the emcee of the most popular variety show in the history of television, and he was always on the look-out for new talent. By chance, Sullivan had been at London's Heathrow Airport the day the Beatles returned from a five-day tour of Sweden. He had seen hundreds of fans scream in unison when the Beatles stepped off their plane and on the spot, he had made up his mind to ask them to appear on his show. Now, in his meetings with Brian, Ed Sullivan engaged the Beatles for two appearances, on February 9 and 16, 1964. Sullivan agreed to pay them $3500 per show, plus the cost of their air fare. And reluctantly, he agreed to give them top billing on the show.

On this same trip to New York, Brian personally took a copy of "I Want to Hold Your Hand" to Capitol and played it for the executives. They were unenthusiastic about the song but since the Beatles' appearance on "The Ed Sullivan Show" would give them national exposure, they agreed to press 200,000 copies. When the record surprisingly started to be played on the radio, Capitol upped the number to 1,000,000. It was a smart move. On January 25, "I Want to Hold Your Hand" hit number one on the charts.

Capitol now made a 180-degree turn and went all out to publicize the Beatles before their arrival in February. Posters reading "The Beatles are coming" turned up everywhere. Disc jockeys were given taped interviews with the Beatles to play on the air and because their songs were on different labels and were all out at once, the Beatles had four singles on the best-seller charts.

On the day of the Beatles' arrival, fans were offered free T-shirts to go to the airport to greet them. Five thousand people showed up in the cold, blustery weather and as the Beatles stepped out of the plane, the fans serenaded them with the song, "We Love You Beatles." The Beatles were astonished by the size of the crowd and by the number of reporters covering their arrival, which had generated as much excitement as an alien landing in a B-grade science fiction movie. For John, who had idolized so many American rock stars, it was a dream come true.

For the rest of their U.S. visit, the Beatles were mobbed everywhere they went. Cynthia, who was accompanying John on tour for the first time, was caught in the middle of a crowd outside the Plaza Hotel in New York, where they were staying. John had to shout for the police to help her, but even they were unable to get her through the crowd. Finally they lifted her over the heads of the fans and threw her into the limousine. As she landed on John's lap, he snapped, "Don't be so slow. They could have killed you." John was terrified that the fans would stampede or crush them, and he and Cynthia went to great lengths to avoid them. They once left the Plaza through the kitchen and climbed into a meat wagon among the hinds of beef—just to go out on the town.

On Sunday, February 9, over 400 girls in the audience of the "Ed Sullivan Show" shrieked simultaneously when the Beatles stepped onto the stage. Ed Sullivan read them a telegram congratulating the Beatles on their success in the United States. The telegram was from Elvis Presley! More than 73 million people at home watched as they sang "Till There Was You," "She Loves You" and "I Want to Hold Your Hand." When the cameras focused on each Beatle his name appeared on the screen. Beneath John's name was the added message, "Sorry girls, he's married."—news that prompted hundreds of girls to write begging him to divorce Cynthia.

In reviewing the Beatles' performance on "The Ed Sullivan Show" the critic from *Newsweek* criticized their appearance and their music: "Musically they are a near disaster: guitars and drums slamming out a merciless beat that does away with secondary rhythms, harmony and melody. Their lyrics (punctuated by nutty shouts of yeah, yeah, yeah!) are a catastrophe. . . ."

*For millions of Americans, this was
their introduction to John Lennon (right)
and the Beatles—as they appeared on
"The Ed Sullivan Show" in 1964.*

But the teenagers disagreed. They loved the loud, driving beat and they liked the simple lyrics about love. Most of all, they loved the Beatles' hair. Overnight Beatlemania spread across the United States. Two months after the Beatles' appearances on "The Ed Sullivan Show" their new single "Can't Buy Me Love" sold so many advance copies that it entered the charts in the number one position. In the United States the top five songs were all Beatles records:

1. Can't Buy Me Love
2. Twist and Shout
3. She Loves You
4. I Want to Hold Your Hand
5. Please Please Me

The Beatles' success in the United States paved the way for the British "invasion." Previously, British groups and singers had failed to make a dent in the American music world, but now they became the rage. The majority faded fast, but some—like the Rolling Stones, the Kinks, the Moody Blues, and the Who—endured to the eighties.

To attract attention, the groups that followed the Beatles were louder and raunchier and the songs they sang, like the Rolling Stones' "(I Can't Get No) Satisfaction," were openly sexual. The "bad boy" image of the Stones sharply contrasted with the Beatles. Only John's closest friends knew he was as much a rebel and "bad boy" as Mick Jagger, the lead singer of the Rolling Stones. Privately, John was very much like Mick and they were good friends. The Stones' first hit was a Lennon/McCartney song, "I Wanna Be Your Man."

The British invasion left its mark on other areas of American culture as well as music. British fashions such as white lipstick and mini-skirts took over the fashion scene. British movie stars such as Michael Caine reached the height of their popularity, and London became THE place to go. For a while Great Britain again ruled American culture.

THE TOURING YEARS

7

Because of the Beatles' success in the United States, they were heavily booked around the world. John's life was dominated by the group's grueling tours from 1964 until 1966. In 1964 alone the Beatles toured Holland, Scandinavia, Japan, Australia, New Zealand, and the United States—but the American tour was the longest and the most successful. They performed in twenty-three cities, breaking box office records everywhere. Quickly, however, it became meaningless to all of them, especially to John. He was bored by the same questions, the same food, the same screaming in city after city. He often asked Brian, "Where am I?"

Pressured by their schedule and the monotony of the tours, the Beatles' performances became puppet-like. Sometimes the screaming was so loud that the Beatles only mouthed the words. The audience never noticed.

Unable to go out sightseeing without getting mobbed, the Beatles stayed in their hotel rooms, playing cards, telling jokes or writing new songs. To ease their boredom, they smoked marijuana almost daily. Once, when asked if they felt like caged animals, John quipped, "No, we feed ourselves." Yet, in a sense, they were trapped and their lives closely resembled the plot of their first movie, *A Hard Day's Night.*

In this film, the Beatles played four lovable, cheerful rock stars pursued by their fans all over London. They evade their fans, but the next day they are captured at the recording studio. Ringo then escapes alone and goes to a park where he is caught and dragged back to the studio by John, Paul, and George.

The movie was not much of an exaggeration. During the shooting John was besieged by fans who gathered all day long to watch the filming and to ask for autographs. At night when he arrived home he was besieged again by dozens of young girls gathered at his door. As he struggled to unlock the door and get inside, they screamed at him and tore off his ties and scarves as souvenirs. He often staggered in and told Cynthia, "I had no idea it was going to be like this. It's a madhouse out there."

To escape fans, John and Cynthia bought a mock Tudor mansion in the countryside outside London. At the same time, John bought Mimi a secluded bungalow overlooking the sea because fans were also flocking to her house begging for souvenirs. He also gave Mimi a plaque to hang over her fireplace. It read, "The guitar's all very well, John, but you'll never make a *living* of it."

John was already a millionaire and he spent money freely. He completely furnished his new house, built a swimming pool and a recording studio, hired a chauffeur to drive his Rolls Royce and a housekeeper to help Cynthia.

"It was a time of utter extravagance," said Cynthia. Only two years earlier they had been nearly penniless and their new wealth thrilled them. They bought cameras, clothes, antiques, crystal, silverware, even a $10,000 horsedrawn carriage and eight white horses for Julian. They went on vacation to exotic places like Tahiti. In the midst of his riches, though, John longed for simple pleasures. He wanted to go to a pub for a glass of beer or to the movies like an average man. During the height of Beatlemania, the Beatles sang that money "Can't Buy Me Love." John probably wanted to sing that it "can't buy me privacy," either.

On the tours it was even worse than at home. The Beatles returned to the United States for a second tour in 1965, and it was a repeat of the first. Day after day for week after week they were trapped in their hotel rooms, and night after night they performed in arenas like Shea Stadium in New York, where they were drowned out by the audience's screams. When John was asked why he stopped singing "Twist and Shout" on stage, he replied, "We'd been doing it for years. It was starting to sicken us."

When the Beatles were on tour, they were together twenty-four hours a day. It was like living in a crowded cocoon and soon John felt he was losing his identity. He thought, "I'm no good. I'm not talented. I can't do anything but be a Beatle." He started to see himself as John Beatle, not John Lennon. Of the four, John was the one who was most afraid that he would not succeed on his own, and he expressed his inner insecurity in songs like "I'm a Loser." In it he hints that "what you see is not the real me."

Home from a European tour, John breaks into a Flamenco dance as the Beatles arrive at London's Heathrow airport. Delighted fans fill the galleries to greet their idols.

Yet John did establish his own identity with the public through his book, *John Lennon: In His Own Write.* Published in 1964, this thin book of verses, cartoons, and short short stories satirizes government and religion. Mimi called the book "just his scribble," but the critics praised its caustic wit, its sense of the ridiculous, and its puns such as "dancing with wild abdomen." John's style of writing was compared to Edward Lear's nonsense poetry, and the *New York Times* called the book "irreverent" and "hilarious." But *In His Own Write* revealed the dark side of John's humor and personality, the side Brian kept hidden from the press and the public. For example, in the poem "Good Dog Nigel," John praised the good qualities of the dog but ended with the line ". . . we're putting you to sleep at three of the clock, Nigel." The book reviewer for *Newsweek* wrote that "seemingly when Lennon sings 'I Want to Hold Your Hand' he is wishing he could bite it."

In 1965, John's second book, *A Spaniard in the Works*, was published. It was similar to the first, and was also well received. Despite the critical and commercial success of these books, John's feelings of insecurity continued and surfaced again in the song "Help!", the title song of their second movie.

The plot of *Help!* centered around a scheme to steal a sacred ring from Ringo's finger. The action followed the Beatles from country to country, chased by a mad scientist and members of a fanatical Eastern cult. Most of the critics felt that both the movie and the soundtrack were inferior to *A Hard Day's Night*, although they did receive favorable reviews. *Time* magazine said that "the charm and experimental spontaneity of *A Hard Day's Night* has been replaced by highly professional, carefully calculated camera work and cutting." The review also said that "as actors they are still nothing but Beatles, without enough characterization—or even caricaturization—to play anything but sight gags."

John, however, disliked *Help!* because he felt the Beatles were not themselves in it. He said, "It was like having clams in a movie about frogs."

The mad pursuit of the Beatles in *Help!* was rather like the mad pursuit by their fans during their tours, which John described as "one big mess." But John was restless at home between tours. His home life had almost ceased to exist while he was on the road and Cynthia was at home caring for Julian, and now he sometimes went for days without talking to her. He could spend entire days curled up on a sofa doing nothing. "Nowhere Man" was a description of how he felt during this period.

At home, John forgot the hassles of the tours and remembered only the highlights. So, in 1966, he and the other Beatles agreed to tour the United States for the third time. It was their last tour. The tour started off on a sour note. In an interview with a London newspaper, John had made some controversial remarks about Christianity which were reprinted in the teen magazine *Datebook* in the United States. Asked his views on organized religion, John had said, "Christianity will go. It will vanish and shrink. I needn't argue about that. I'm right and I will be proved right. We're more popular than Jesus now. I don't know which will go first—rock and roll or Christianity. Jesus was all right but his disciples were thick and ordinary. It's them twisting it that ruins it for me."

As always, John had been outspoken and arrogant, but in Great Britain his comments were all but unnoticed. In the United States, on the other hand, his comments were called "blasphemous" by some Americans. Several conservative religious leaders organized anti-Beatle demonstrations where people burned or pulverized Beatles albums and several radio stations banned their songs.

Hate mail and death threats poured into the Beatles' office. Brian feared for John's life and wanted to cancel their upcoming tour. But John insisted that the Beatles make the

In spite of John's controversial comments on Christianity, thousands of fans packed Chicago's International Amphitheater for this Beatles concert on their final U.S. tour in 1966.

tour as scheduled. He was greatly upset and bewildered by the anger and the hatred that he had aroused and he wanted to rectify it. Looking tired and nervous, he apologized at a press conference in Chicago. "I'm sorry I said it, really, I never meant it to be a lousy anti-religious thing. From what I've read, or observed, Christianity just seems to be shrinking, to be losing contact."

He also said, "I'm not anti-God, anti-Christ or anti-religion. I was not saying we are greater or better. I believe in God, but not as one thing, not as an old man in the sky. I believe that what people call God is something in all of us." Despite his apology, garbage was thrown at the Beatles on stage in Memphis, and wherever they went there were anti-Beatle signs hanging next to those that read "Beatles Forever."

When the Beatles ran onto the stage in San Francisco, their last stop, they knew they would never tour again. Ringo summed up the tour years for all of them: "It was the worst time and the best time of my life. The best time because we played a lot of good music and had a lot of good times. The worst time [because it was] twenty-four hours a day, without a break: press, people fighting to get into your hotel rooms, climbing up twenty-five stories of drainpipes. And it never stopped. . . . If it had carried on, I personally would have gone insane."

THE MUSIC
AND
ITS MEANING

8

Question: How do you rate your music?
John: We're not good musicians, just adequate.
Question: Then why are you so popular?
John: Maybe people like adequate music.

John's put-down of the Beatles' music at a press conference in Japan in '64 was a typical self-mocking quip, which neither the fans nor he took seriously. In the world of rock music, the Beatles' contribution was extraordinary and they were phenomenally successful. According to the *Guiness Book of World Records*, the Beatles earned a record of 42 gold discs, which are awarded for sales of more than 1,000,000. They also hold the record for number one hits with an astounding 20 top songs to their credit.

The Beatles' initial success was as much a result of their image and their wit as their pounding bass beat. They put joy and exuberance into simple love songs like "She Loves You" and presented the world with a fun-loving foursome. But what kept them on top for ten years and insured their legendary success was their ability to mirror the times in their songs through originality and growth. As the principal songwriters, John and Paul led the group, moving from the simple message of "I Want to Hold Your Hand" to complex songs of social comment, such as "Eleanor Rigby" and "A Day in the Life."

John and Paul share the credit for the wide variety of songs the Beatles recorded, and their collaboration was especially close in the early '60s. They sometimes sat at a piano for hours playing chords and testing lyrics. Neither John nor Paul read or wrote music so they put their songs on tape.

It was John, however, who really pushed the Beatles into experimenting and who made the most musical innovations. Although he was less ambitious than Paul, John was spurred on by the competition that existed between them. When "A Hard Day's Night" was chosen as the title of their first movie, the director, Dick Lester, told John. "The next morning," said John, "I brought in the song ["A Hard Day's Night"]. 'Cause there was a little competition between Paul and I as to who got the A side, who got the hit singles. In the early days the majority of the singles—in the movies and everything—were mine . . . either my song, or my voice, or both." Generally the writer of the song sang it, but "A Hard Day's Night" was an exception because John was unable to reach the high notes in the chorus. Later John wrote some songs specifically for George or Ringo to sing.

In the mid-sixties John met the popular singer Bob Dylan and was strongly influenced by him. Dylan, who was known for his protest songs, told John, "Pay attention to the words." He encouraged John to write songs in the same style as his book *In His Own Write*. By 1964 John no longer felt it was necessary to write simple songs for the mass market, or as he called it, "the meat market." Following Dylan's advice, he did begin to write songs that were similar in style to his verses in *In His Own Write*, songs whose lyrics were more personal and more complex. The songs "I'm a Loser" and "I'll Cry Instead" were personal and biting—evidence of a new direction in John's music. Many music critics called him the most literate of all rock writers.

Paul's songs also grew more complex in the mid-sixties and George Martin, their record producer, said that "Paul learned about words from John." Together John and Paul reached the peak of their collaboration in 1967 with "A Day in the Life," which was on the album *Sgt. Pepper's Lonely Hearts Club Band*. A melancholy song about the futility of man's existence, it was compared to T.S. Eliot's poem, "The Waste Land." Nevertheless, Paul continued to write primarily ballads and classic rock songs such as "Yesterday," "Michelle," and "I'm Down." Paul's songs were more popular with the general public and were recorded more often by other artists such as Frank Sinatra.

At the same time that John's lyrics were changing, his songs also showed a steady musical progression. As early as 1964, he experimented with unusual sounds. For example, his single "I Feel Fine" opens with a strange buzzing noise that sounds like a chainsaw. The sound was the feedback from an electric guitar, and it paved the way for the acid rock sound of the Who, Jimi Hendrix, and the Jefferson Starship.

The album *Rubber Soul* (1965) was a milestone which expanded the boundaries of rock 'n' roll by the effective use of unusual instruments such as the sitar, a twenty-one-string instrument from India. The Beatles had used a sitar before on the LP "Help!" but much less effectively than in John's song "Norwegian Wood." George played the sitar on some of the Beatles' recordings. By combining various forms of music, Bob Dylan said, the Beatles "were doing things no one else was doing." Just as he had influenced John's writing, Dylan in his turn was greatly influenced by the Beatles. This influence led him to write the first folk-rock songs, such as "Mr. Tambourine Man."

Beginning with *Rubber Soul*, the Beatles took charge of designing their album covers, many of which reflected John's unconventional thinking. John, for example, originated the idea for their infamous and repulsive "butcher cover" on *The Beatles—Yesterday and Today*, an album consisting of songs from *Rubber Soul* and *Help!* The Beatles wanted to protest the recycling or butchering of their albums so they posed for the cover photograph in white butchers' overalls, surrounded by bloody meat bones and limbless dolls. The cover was attacked by disc jockeys as soon as the LP was released, with the result that Capitol recalled the albums and inserted the records in new sleeves.

The Beatles took their music another step in *Revolver* (1966). Although it was released before their last American tour, the Beatles never sang any of the songs on it. The musical arrangements used synthesized music and electronic distortion which were impossible to duplicate on the stage. For instance, the yawn-like sound in John's song "I'm Only Sleeping" was created by playing a taped guitar passage backwards.

With *Revolver*, the group abandoned the "Beatle sound," and the songs on the album are individualized according to the style of the person who wrote or sang it. John, in particular, experimented with unique effects. George Martin said that for "Tomorrow Never Knows" John wanted "his voice to sound atmospheric. We laid down the track with Ringo on drums and a tamboura drone, and I put John's voice through a Leslie speaker to make a weird noise." Martin was frequently responsible for devising ways to create the sounds and the effects that John and Paul wanted, because as untrained musicians, they sometimes asked for the impossible—such as violins playing the note C.

Except for "Eleanor Rigby," a Lennon/McCartney collaboration, the songs on *Revolver* were written individually and John's songs, such as "She Said, She Said" and "Tomorrow Never Knows," are reflections of his experiences with the psychedelic drug LSD. John and George and their wives, Patti and Cynthia, were unknowingly slipped LSD at a dinner party in 1965. It was the first time they had taken the drug, and they were terrified by the hallucinations it caused. They ran away from the party and went into London, but their hallucinations became worse. John thought the red lights he saw were raging fires. A few months later, however, he wanted to "see" and "hear" unusual sights and sounds and he took LSD voluntarily. The drug soon became an escape from depression and insecurity, and in a *Rolling Stone* interview in 1971, he said, "I ate it all the time."

George occasionally used LSD, and at John's urging, Ringo and Paul tried it a few times. They all entered a psychedelic period at the same time, wearing bright, colorful, flowered shirts, baggy pants, longer hair, and sneakers or sandals. John even painted psychedelic designs on his Rolls Royce.

LSD, or "acid," played an important role in the formation of the counter-culture movement. Thousands of young people turned on to drugs and "dropped out" of the mainstream of society. Of all the Beatles, John was most in tune with the students who were dropping out because he had always been a rebel, and he now became the figurehead leader of the counter-culture. In 1967 *Newsweek* conducted a poll of students on 38 college campuses asking them to name their heroes or leaders. The "most popular non-ideological idols" were the Beatles, and John's name was listed in particular. His songs such as "Strawberry Fields Forever" expressed the confusion of the younger generation in lines such as "It's all right. . . . But it's all wrong, that is . . ." Young people were searching for a solution to the world's problems and the Beatles' song "All You Need Is Love" gave them a simple answer. The summer of 1967 became known as the "summer of love," a time when young people carried flowers as a symbol of peace and love, sang "All You Need Is Love" and dropped out to live in "hippie" communes.

At the height of the counter-culture movement the Beatles released their album *Sgt. Pepper's Lonely Hearts Club Band*, which captured the mood and spirit of the times with songs like "She's Leaving Home" and "With a Little Help from My Friends." The first Beatle LP to be built around a theme, *Sgt. Pepper* blended each song into the next as the imaginary character Sgt. Pepper led a cabaret show. It combined elements of jazz, classical music, rock, blues, and avant-garde or experimental music. *Sgt. Pepper* received rave reviews. *Time* magazine said it transformed rock into "an art form," and the newspaper the *Village Voice* called it "the most ambitious and most successful record album ever issued." It was also the most analyzed.

All of the songs on *Sgt. Pepper* were scrutinized for hidden meanings and references to drugs. Earlier songs like "Day Tripper" had shown the Beatles were part of the drug culture and nearly all of the songs on *Sgt. Pepper* were interpreted as odes to drugs: "friends" in "I Get High with a Little Help from My Friends" was interpreted as "uppers" while "Fixing a Hole" was interpreted as injecting heroin. John called the interpretations ridiculous. Yet not only acrostic lovers, but music critics, fans, and religious leaders quickly noted that the initials of his song "Lucy in the Sky with Diamonds" are LSD. They also pointed out that the images in the song are psychedelic:

> Picture yourself in a boat on a river
> With tangerine trees and marmalade skies . . .

With increasing sarcasm, John insisted the song was not inspired by LSD but by a picture his son Julian drew and described as "lucy in the sky with diamonds." Despite his reputation for honesty, no one believed him because just a month before *Sgt. Pepper* was released Paul had admitted taking LSD in an interview in *Life* magazine. Although critics and fans were convinced that LSD inspired "Lucy in the Sky with Diamonds," the song's theme of drifting in a boat as wonders unfold on the shore is a popular one in literature. Lewis Carroll used it in *Alice in Wonderland*, a work that had often influenced John's writing. Because of the beautiful pictures he painted with his words in "Lucy," John was called a dream weaver.

The analysis of *Sgt. Pepper* was not limited to the music; even the pop art cover of the album received its share of comment. The cover showed a funeral scene with the four Beatles, dressed in satin uniforms and sporting moustaches, standing in front of a grave. On the top of the grave, flowers spelled out, "The Beatles." Marijuana plants grew near the grave, and the Beatles were surrounded by a collage of faces of cult figures such as Marlon Brando, Bob Dylan, Laurel and Hardy, H. G. Wells, and others. Off to the left were wax figures of the Beatles at a younger age, a symbol that was interpreted to mean they were abandoning their former identities. Some observers also said it showed they were abandoning drugs, and this interpretation was given credence when the Beatles made a dramatic change in their lives.

During the summer George, who had become very interested in Eastern philosophy and religion, introduced the others to the Maharishi Mahesh Yogi, a well-known Indian guru

John (right) and Ringo on their way to Wales to hear the Maharishi Mahesh Yogi explain the secrets of transcendental meditation.

and proponent of transcendental meditation, or "TM." The Maharishi invited them to attend a weekend TM workshop in Wales, and as a result of the experience the Beatles publicly announced they were giving up drugs and turning to meditation as their way to get high and find inner peace. John said, "If we'd met the Maharishi before we had taken LSD, we wouldn't have needed to take it."

Ironically, the same weekend the Beatles denounced drugs, Brian Epstein was found dead in his bedroom and the coroner ruled that he had died from the cumulative effect of "incautious self-overdoses" of the sleeping pill Carbitrol. Although the Beatles had known that their manager used drugs, they were not aware that he took even more than they. John was deeply upset because he and Brian had been very close, and Brian had been Julian's godfather.

In the aftermath of Brian's death, John followed George's lead, turning to TM, Eastern religion and Eastern philosophy as a way to discover the meaning of his life. He had failed to ease his pain through drugs, but now, according to Cynthia, the thought of getting high and feeling good without drugs stimulated John's imagination. Cynthia was relieved when John gave up LSD because it had put a barrier between them. She had taken the drug a few times, but her trips had been bad so she refused to continue. If John and Cynthia's marriage had suffered during the years of touring, John's use of drugs had strained it to the breaking point.

In the spring of 1968 John and the other Beatles plus an entourage of their wives, lovers, and friends went to Rishikesh, India for a three-month transcendental meditation course given by the Maharishi. None of them finished it. Ringo and his wife Maureen left after 10 days; Paul and his girlfriend after a month. John, Cynthia, George, and George's wife Patti stayed for two months, living in modest buildings, eating vegetarian food and meditating. Then suddenly John insisted that they leave because he had heard a rumor that the

Maharishi had attempted to seduce one of his students. John was bitterly disillusioned that this spiritual leader should be subject to human weaknesses. When the Maharishi asked him why they were leaving, John sarcastically replied, ''You're the cosmic one, you ought to know . . .''

John returned home depressed and angry. Cynthia now knew she had lost the opportunity to communicate with him, and her hope for saving their marriage was crushed. A few months later it dissolved completely when John fell in love with Yoko Ono.

JOHN AND YOKO
9

John met Yoko Ono in 1966 at the Indica art gallery in London, where she was showing her work. At the time, Yoko was creating a stir in the art world with her experimental or avant-garde art works and films such as "Bottoms," which was a fast-paced film of people's behinds. Like other avant-garde artists of the sixties, she was known for creating art that was shocking. When John entered the gallery, Yoko was putting the final touches on her exhibit "Unfinished Paintings and Objects," and she ignored him.

John wandered through the gallery on his own. The first work of art he saw was an apple—just a plain, ordinary apple—sitting on a pedestal. Next to it was a price tag for £200 ($600). He thought it was hilarious for an artist to display such a "work of art" and to ask an enormous price for it. Next he climbed up a ladder to look at a black canvas that was hanging from the ceiling. On a hook next to it was a pair of binoculars and he peered through them. In tiny letters on the canvas was the word "yes." He was enthralled because the simple "yes" contrasted with the mostly negative avant-garde artwork of the 1960s. As he walked around, Yoko approached him and instead of speaking, she handed him a card reading, "Breathe." He liked the small, off-beat artist at once.

Yoko was born in Japan on February 18, 1933. Born to wealthy parents, she attended exclusive private schools until World War II broke out. During the war she was sent into the countryside with the servants who abandoned her, and she was forced to forage for food. Following the war, she attended Gakushuin University in Tokyo. In 1951 her family emigrated to the United States, and she was sent to Sarah Lawrence College in New York, where she studied art and classical music. She left before graduation to marry a Japanese musician, Toshi Ichiyanagi. Yoko and Toshi lived in New York City, in Greenwich Village—the district famous in the 1950s for its artists and "beatniks." It was here that Yoko first became involved in avant-garde art. She and Toshi divorced in 1964 after seven years of living on and off with each other, and she married Tony Cox, an American movie director. They had a daughter named Kyoko and had just settled in London a few months before she met John.

John and Yoko shared many of the same ideas and interests, and they became good friends very quickly. She often sent John her poems, and she sent him a copy of her "book" *Grapefruit*—a collection of poems printed on cards. Some of her "poems" consisted of one word like "Bleed"; others were instructions for creating "events" or happenings.

Cynthia was amused by Yoko's unusual "art" and "poems." Although she and John were drifting apart, she was not jealous of Yoko in the beginning because John and Yoko were only friends.

John and Yoko found the same things humorous and shared the same sense of the ridiculous; they began going to art galleries together. John even financed her exhibit, "Half a

you are here

Wind Show," that consisted of several commonplace objects such as chairs all cut in half and painted white. John and Yoko also took LSD together and as John and Cynthia grew farther apart, he fell in love with Yoko.

Following their return from India, John and Cynthia separated. Cynthia moved out of their house with Julian and Yoko moved in, leaving her daughter with her husband, Tony Cox. John's fans and even the other Beatles blamed Yoko for breaking up his marriage. In her autobiography, *A Twist of Lennon*, Cynthia wrote that John needed encouragement and support for his way-out ideas and Yoko gave it to him. At the same time Yoko boosted his ego because he respected her enormously and felt that she wouldn't love a "dummy." In these ways, Yoko helped bring him out of his depression.

Encouraged by Yoko, John immediately launched himself into creating avant-garde art works and experimental records. In July 1968, he exhibited his artwork at a gallery in London. In imitation of Yoko's earlier works, his were white. One was a huge round canvas which was all white except for the words printed on it: "You are here." This message showed up at the exhibit again when John announced on the opening day that he and Yoko were planning to get married, although neither of them was legally divorced yet. To celebrate their engagement, John released 360 white helium-filled balloons saying, "I declare these balloons high." Inside each balloon was the message "You are here. Please write to John Lennon, c/o Robert Fraser Gallery." Many people

At an exhibition of John's avant-garde artworks, Yoko Ono admires her friend's round white canvas bearing the words "You are here."

wrote to him to condemn his lifestyle. Nor was this the only criticism John received during the show. Near the door of the art gallery was John's white upturned hat with a sign reading, "For the artist." A group of college students contemptuously put an old rusty bike on top of it, but John made the bike part of the exhibit! The critics, however, shared the students' opinion about the exhibit and panned it.

John and Yoko's experimental or avant-garde albums were also panned. Their first album, *Unfinished Music, No. 1: Two Virgins*, which was recorded in an all-night session in John's home studio, was a cacophony of bird calls, burps, Yoko's screams, and the songs "Together," and "Hush a Bye Hush a Bye." The LP was widely ridiculed, but its cover made it infamous. On the sleeve of *Two Virgins* were full-length nude photographs of John and Yoko which John had taken with his own camera. When he told the executives of EMI that he wanted to use the nude photographs, they had refused to release the album. Along with the other Beatles, they said the cover design was ridiculous. But John insisted that the nude photographs were "art" and in order to have his way, he released the album in the United States through a small company named Tetragrammaton. It was released in England through the Beatles' own company Apple. Since nudity was less accepted in the 1960s than it is today, record stores wrapped *Two Virgins* in small brown bags to avoid charges of obscenity. In response, John and Yoko formed their own company—Bag Productions.

Some people saw the cover of *Two Virgins* as a daring and courageous act, and they took John at his word when he said it was an expression of their love for each other. Many more people, however, thought the cover was tasteless, obscene or foolish. A singer named Rainbo even recorded a novelty song about it entitled "John You Went Too Far This Time." John and Yoko were mocked and ridiculed for their physical appearance, he for knobby knees and she for sagging breasts. John was told that he should have used a photograph of Paul in the nude because he's better looking. John later admitted he had wanted to shock people and had expected some criticism. But he never expected the personal attacks. He was very hurt because people laughed at Yoko's body and called her ugly.

Their next album, *Unfinished Music, No. 2: Life with the Lions*, was also widely criticized for its contents and its cover. Both contents and cover were autobiographical and recorded two traumatic events that had occurred in their lives: their arrest in October 1968 for possession of marijuana and Yoko's miscarriage in November. When John and Yoko were arrested, he swore that they were no longer using marijuana and that it had been planted. However, he pleaded guilty to avoid a trial because Yoko was pregnant and frail. Yoko suffered a miscarriage nonetheless in her seventh month of pregnancy. While she was in the hospital, John never left her side, sleeping on the floor next to her bed.

On the front cover of *Life with the Lions* was a photograph of John sleeping on the floor of the hospital. On the back of the cover was a photograph of John and Yoko at the time of their arrest, looking pale and frightened and surrounded by fourteen burly policemen. Side A of the record was devoted to Yoko's screeching, which was matched by John's screeching guitar feedback. On side B were "No Bed for Beatle John," "Baby's Heartbeat," recorded before Yoko miscarried, and "Two Minutes of Silence." In the United States *Life with the Lions* never rose higher than number 174 on *Billboard* magazine's record charts. During the same period, however, John was also recording with the Beatles, and their albums such as *The Beatles* and *Abbey Road* were selling extremely well and receiving rave reviews.

The notoriety of John and Yoko's albums was matched by the notoriety of their campaign against the Vietnam War in the late 1960s. John had opposed the war for a long time, but because of Brian's instructions not to talk about it, he had not spoken out against the war until after Brian's death. In 1968 John and Yoko began their peace campaign by staging events as symbolic protests. First, they planted two acorns at Coventry Cathedral in London as a symbol of East (Yoko) meeting West (John). Then they announced that they planned to send acorns to the world leaders to plant in the name of peace. The press labeled John and Yoko "Nuts for Peace," but hundreds of people helped them in their efforts by sending them acorns. One elderly woman sent two acorns she had saved for forty years, and Golda Meir, the Prime Minister of Israel, was among the world leaders who actually planted the acorns they received.

John and Yoko were married on March 20, 1969 in Gibraltar, and they decided to turn their honeymoon into a "peace event." They invited reporters to a "bed-in" for peace at the Hilton Hotel in Amsterdam, Holland. Some reporters expected to see John and Yoko making love. Instead, they saw them sitting in bed. Signs above the bed read "Bed Peace" and "Hair Peace." They stayed in bed for seven days in the cause of peace and, predictably, many people thought they were ridiculous. John felt that "the least Yoko and I can do is hog the headlines and make people laugh. We're quite willing to be the world's clowns if it will do any good. For reasons known only to themselves, people print what I say. And I say 'peace.'" The interviews John and Yoko gave during their bed-in for peace appeared on the B

On their honeymoon in 1969, John and Yoko held the famous "bed-in" for peace in their suite at the Hilton Hotel in Amsterdam.

side of *The Wedding Album*; the A side consists of twenty-two minutes of them saying and screeching each other's names.

Two months after their wedding, John and Yoko staged their second bed-in in Montreal, Canada. They had originally intended to stage it in the United States, but John was denied a visa. He said, "If I'm a joke as they say, and not important, why don't they just let me in?" On the final day of the Montreal bed-in John and Yoko recorded his new song "Give Peace a Chance" with Timothy Leary, an ex-Harvard professor who had promoted LSD, disc jockey Murray "the K" Kaufman, comedian Tommy Smothers, and the Radha Krishna Temple Singers. "Give Peace a Chance" was probably John's largest contribution to the peace movement because it was used as the rallying cry of anti-war demonstrators. The war had dragged on since the early sixties, and many Americans were beginning to think it was a futile effort. The number of anti-war demonstrations and marches increased daily, and "Give Peace a Chance" was sung at all of them.

As part of their peace campaign, John and Yoko staged "bag-ins" as well as bed-ins. During interviews they wore large bags or huge white pillowcases over their heads. The bag-ins were symbolic gestures to express their belief that many wars are fought because of prejudice. In their opinion, bagism would eliminate pre-judging people by their appearance.

Their bag-ins and bed-ins brought them both boos and cheers. The British newspaper the *Daily Mirror* said that John "seems to have gone completely off his rocker." On the other hand, *Rolling Stone* named John their "Man of the Year" for his contributions to music and peace. At Christmas time John and Yoko plastered posters all over the United States saying, "War is over if you want it. Happy Christmas from John and Yoko." John later said that they received a big response to their posters. "We got just thank you's from lots of youths around the world—for all the things we were doing—that inspired *them* to do something. We had a lot of response from other than pop fans, which was interesting, from all walks of life and age."

John also protested the Vietnam War by returning his MBE medal to Queen Elizabeth. The medal, which represents Membership in the Order of the British Empire, had been awarded to John and the other Beatles for their "services to exports" in 1965. At that time, the Beatles had boosted the sagging British economy through the enormous sale of their records and Beatles products. Normally, the medal is given to military men for heroism and the Beatles receiving the honor created a storm of protest. John created even more of a furor when he returned his.

Although John and Yoko were outwardly calm about the criticism of their bag-ins and bed-ins, they were sensitive to it. John expressed his feelings in the song, "The Ballad of John and Yoko." In it he said that it was hard for Yoko and him to be different, but the line, "Christ! You know it ain't easy" brought yet another protest from religious leaders. Once again John was forced to defend himself. This time he said simply, "I'm Christ's biggest fan."

In addition to the criticism and the poor sales of their records, John and Yoko were confronted with growing tension among the Beatles. Yoko now went everywhere with John, and the other Beatles resented her constant presence. She was even at recording sessions. They were also upset by her influence over John and by the bizarre antics she and John pulled, which they felt hurt the Beatle image.

As a result of their unhappiness, John and Yoko started sniffing heroin and became hooked on it. They kicked the habit, though, after several months, and in his song "Cold Turkey" John wrote about their addiction. The song showed John's courage, for few other major rock stars would have written about the horrors of drug addiction. Yet the song was banned by several radio stations just because it was about drugs.

Paul disliked the bleakness of "Cold Turkey," so he had refused to record it. John then recorded it with Eric Clapton, Klaus Voormann, and Alan White, whom he called the Plastic Ono Band. He credited the song to himself and to the band, thus ending his unwritten agreement with Paul to use Lennon/McCartney as the by-line for all their songs. It was a clear sign that the Beatles were splitting apart.

THE BREAKUP OF THE BEATLES

10

At the end of 1969, John told the other Beatles that he wanted to leave the group, that he wanted a "divorce." However, he agreed not to publicly announce his withdrawal from the group because it would affect their financial deals. But a few months later, Paul made the breakup public through a snide self-interview inserted in copies of his first solo album *McCartney*:

Q: Do you miss the other Beatles and George Martin? . . .

A: No.

Q: Do you foresee a time when Lennon/McCartney becomes an active songwriting partnership again?

A: No.

It was a bitter ending to a group that had accomplished so much together and to a songwriting team which had been compared with the best.

John was particularly angry that the press announced that Paul had quit the group. He told *Rolling Stone* his version of the split: "The cartoon is this—four guys on a stage with a spotlight on them; second picture, three guys on stage breezing out of the spotlight; third picture, one guy standing there shouting 'I'm leaving.' " John saw Paul's melodramatic withdrawal as a publicity gimmick designed to sell albums.

In fact, however, the publicity Paul received was largely negative. *Rolling Stone* asked, ". . . how could he have sunk to such bizarre tactics?" and the breakup became even nastier when Paul sued the others for his official release from the group and their corporation. The public took turns blaming Paul and Yoko for causing the split, but actually it had been all but inevitable since the mid-sixties; they were four boys who grew up and eventually went their separate ways.

As early as 1966 John had wanted to leave the group. Following their last tour, he had accepted a role in the anti-war movie "How I Won the War" in order to get away from the others and to think about his future. By the time the shooting of the movie ended, he had discovered that he missed the Beatles' companionship while he was on location in Spain, and that he lacked the courage to withdraw from the group. Back home in England, John continued to spend most of his time with the others even though the tours had ended. But he was beginning to write on his own, and albums such as *Rubber Soul* and *Revolver* indicate he was going in a different direction from Paul, for John's songs contained psychedelic images and personal statements about himself.

The major change in John's relationship with the others occurred after he met Yoko. He had always leaned toward experimental work in both art and music, and Yoko encouraged him to follow his inclination to create avant-garde works. She was blamed for leading him away from the Beatles, but John himself said, "I was starting to drift away from the Beatles before Yoko. What I did . . . in my own cowardly way was *use* Yoko." As John became more involved with Yoko, he lost interest in the Beatles and he gave up his leadership role. When Brian died, Paul took over as the unofficial leader, but where the others had once accepted John as the leader of the group, they came to resent Paul in this role and felt he was bossy.

The Beatles' first project after Brian's death was *A Magical Mystery Tour*. It was a *cinéma vérité* film of a two-week "mystery" tour of southern England, which Paul had suggested and which, without Brian's organization, had turned into a chaotic mess. But the Beatles persisted. After the shooting was completed, Paul and John edited the footage. They generally worked separately and spent much of their time re-editing each other's work.

The final version of "The Magical Mystery Tour" was aired by the BBC on December 26, 1967. Over fifteen million viewers tuned in to watch it, but most of them were disappointed. The rambling sixty-minute movie lacked the Beatles' usual humor and was as boring as a home movie. The critics were venomous, calling it "sad" and "blatant rubbish." As a result of its poor reviews in England, it was never aired in the United States.

Only two important songs came out of the movie: Paul's "Fool on the Hill" and John's "I Am the Walrus." "Fool on the Hill" expressed the idea that the fool was actually wiser than those around him. "I Am the Walrus" drew its inspiration from Lewis Carroll's poem "The Walrus and the Carpenter" in *Through the Looking-Glass* in which the walrus asks silly questions like "why the sea is boiling hot." John randomly strung thoughts together, and the walrus talked about flights of fancy.

The album was generally panned, with Rex Reed calling it "phony pretentious overcooked tripe."

Their next album, *The Beatles*, was a comeback. Nick-named the "white album" because of its stark white cover, it contained several excellent songs. Yet John said that all the songs on it are "individual tracks. There isn't any Beatle music on it."

Neither Paul nor John made significant contributions to each other's songs on *The Beatles*, so John's songs were harsh, no longer balanced by Paul's sweet tone. His songs were primarily political ones like "Happiness Is a Warm Gun," "Revolution," and "Revolution 9," which consisted of dia-logue, screams, and gunshots. It closely resembled Yoko's songs and the music he was recording with her during the same period. John also wrote autobiographical songs like "Julia," which was about his mother, and "Sexy Sadie," which was a thinly disguised attack on the Maharishi who John felt had betrayed his trust. It was typical of John to use his songs as a release for his emotions and as attacks on his enemies and on things he disliked.

The Beatles was recorded in an atmosphere of tension and strain, caused, in part, by Yoko's presence at the record-ing sessions. She made Paul feel self-conscious, and it was no secret that he and George disliked her. Yet John was so enthralled by her and so impressed by her avant-garde recordings that he expected the others to recognize her intel-ligence and creativity.

In describing the breakup of the Beatles in the magazine *Musician: Player and Listener*, Paul later said, "Friction came in; business things; relations between us. We were all looking for people in our lives. John had found Yoko; it made things very difficult. He wanted a very intense, intimate life with her; at the same time, we'd always reserved that kind of intimacy for the group."

The "business things" Paul referred to were the failure of the Beatles' corporation, Apple, and their quarrel over whom to name as their manager. After Brian's death, the Beatles had decided to manage themselves instead of hiring a professional manager. They set up the company Apple Corps, Ltd. to handle their finances and productions. Its five divisions were Apple Retailing, Apple Electronics, Apple Publishing, Apple Records, and Apple Films.

With great fanfare the retailing division opened the Apple Boutique in London on December 7, 1967. It was stocked with the "hippie" fashions of the day and Art Deco reproductions. John called it a "psychedelic Woolworth's" and he hired his old boyhood friend Pete Shotton to manage it. The Boutique attracted scores of window shoppers but few buyers, and it closed eight months later.

John hired his friend Alexis Mardas to head the electronics division because he was intrigued by Alex's electronic gimmicks. He loved his "nothing box," which randomly flashed a series of small red lights on and off. Sitting alone at home, John sometimes stared at it for hours and tried to guess which light would flash on next. Alex worked feverishly in the lab of Apple Electronics, but he never produced a single item that was workable or salable.

The movie and publishing divisions were also failures, and although the record division was successful, it did not make enough money to offset the losses of the other four divisions.

In the spring John told the magazine *Disc and Music Echo*, "Apple is losing money at the rate of £18,000-£20,000 ($54,000-$60,000) a week. If it carries on like this, I'll personally be broke in six months."

Apple Corps lost money because of poor management and foolish spending. John had even hired an astrologer to cast horoscopes for the staff.

Finally, in late 1968, the Beatles decided to hire a manager, but John and Paul disagreed on who it should be. John lobbied for the Rolling Stones' former manager Allan Klein who had a reputation as a shrewd businessman and a wheel-er-dealer. Paul wanted to hire Lee Eastman, an American lawyer whose daughter Linda Paul later married. George sided with John in the dispute and the three of them signed a contract with Klein. When Paul signed a separate contract with Eastman, the group unofficially split.

In a futile attempt to recapture the relationship of their early years together and the spirit of their early performances, the Beatles started work on the film "Let It Be." The project drove them further apart. For John the three weeks of filming were "misery." He tolerated it in order for the Beatles to fulfill their three-movie contract with United Artists. (They had previously recorded a third soundtrack album for the animated "Yellow Submarine," but United Artists insisted that the Beatles had to star in three movies.)

"Let It Be," originally titled "Get Back," was a documentary of the Beatles at work. It revealed the boredom and bickering of the Beatles, including a bitter argument between Paul and George. Throughout the filming John was stoned and indifferent. Yoko was depressed because she was recovering from injuries she had received in a car accident. In his attempt to take control over the project, Paul was bossy and critical and John later said, "The film was set up by Paul, for Paul." Only the final scene of a concert on the rooftop of the Apple building captures the Beatles of old, playing with enthusiasm as hundreds gather below to listen. At the end of their performance, John said, "I hope we passed the audition."

The soundtrack of "Let It Be" was a mediocre album. It contained only three songs that achieved the Beatles' former standards: Paul's "Get Back" and "Let It Be" and John's "Across the Universe." The entire LP was poorly recorded because John wanted to capture the perfect track for each song live, that is on one take without production gimmicks. It was a task that greatly increased the frustration and tension of the group. At first John wanted to scrap the album, but then he changed his mind and hired Phil Spector to re-mix it. Spector's "wall of sound" contrasted with the simple style John had demanded from George Martin, and as a result, two incompatible styles were combined on the final LP. The release of *Let It Be* was held up to coincide with the premiere of the movie.

Meanwhile, the Beatles recorded *Abbey Road.* In spite of the discord within the group, it was a polished, snappy album that reflected their varied styles and innovations. John's contributions to it were slight, however, because he was deeply involved in his peace campaign and his album with Yoko. His most popular song on Abbey Road was "Come Together!" a rousing plea for harmony among people.

On May 20, 1970 the premiere of "Let It Be" was held in London. None of the Beatles attended it because Paul had announced the breakup of the group in April. Alan Smith, critic for *New Musical Express*, wrote that "Let It Be" was "a sad and tatty end to a musical fusion which wiped clean and drew again the forces of pop music." He was right. But as George Martin said, "It's amazing to me . . . that they didn't break up earlier under the strain of superstardom. They were living in a golden prison all the time, living with each other and not growing into individual lives. Now they're living individual lives and enjoying it."

THE
SOLO YEARS

11

After the Beatles split up, John said, "The dream is over. It's over and we gotta—well, I have anyway, personally, get down to so-called reality." He made the comment in *Rolling Stone* on December 31, 1970, but it took him several years to face reality and find himself.

John expected to feel liberated when the Beatles broke up. Instead he felt lost and for help he turned to "primal therapy," which he had learned about from Dr. Arthur Janov's book, *The Primal Scream*. John was fascinated by the concept of primal therapy in which the patient relives unhappy moments in his or her life and then relieves the tension and anxiety of the painful process by screaming. John decided to undergo the therapy—after all, Yoko's screams and shrieks were famous.

For six months John and Yoko went to the Primal Institute in Los Angeles, California, which was run by Dr. Janov. John "relived" traumatic moments such as the death of his mother, and said the experience taught him to cry. But John left the Institute angry and disturbed because Dr. Janov wanted to film the session he and Yoko were attending. John saw it as an attempt to use him to gain recognition for the Institute. He later said in a *Playboy* interview, "At first I was bitter about Maharishi being human and bitter about Janov being human. Well, I'm not bitter anymore. . . . I meditate and I cry."

Primal therapy left its mark on John's next album *John Lennon/Plastic Ono Band*, nicknamed the "Primal album." In the song "Mother," which climaxed with a shrill scream, he wrote: "Mother you had me, but I never had you." In "Working Class Hero" he wrote about the pain of growing up in the working class and in "God" he listed many of the people and things that had disappointed him in life, the Bible, Elvis Presley, Bob Dylan, John F. Kennedy, ending with the lines, "I don't believe in Beatles/I just believe in me." Actually, he was still struggling to find himself and he was still bitter about the way the Beatles had broken up. In the song "I Found Out" John continued the attack he had begun in "God" and lashed out at all the methods he had tried in his quest for inner peace: transcendental meditation, Eastern religion, drugs, and more.

In his next album, *Imagine*, John made a vicious attack on Paul in the song "How Do You Sleep?" He described Paul's songs as "Muzak" and continued, "You must have learned something in all those years." The attack on Paul was made even nastier by the inclusion of a postcard on which John is holding a pig by the ears, a spoof of the photograph of Paul holding a sheep by the ears on the cover of his LP, *Rams*.

The title song "Imagine," on the other hand, is a mellow song inspired by Yoko's "imagine" poems in her book *Grapefruit*. It's one of John Lennon's most popular and respected songs and one of the few post-Beatles songs that is on a par with those from the Beatle era. In it he asks the listener to imagine a utopian world—a world without hunger, war, greed, or even countries. The inclusion of "Imagine" and "How Do You Sleep?" on the same album is a striking example of the dichotomy of John's personality. He was often violent and vindictive, yet he was a champion for world peace. He was cynical and sarcastic, yet he was also an idealist.

Imagine was followed by John's worst album, *Some Time in New York City.* In the months before the album was recorded he and Yoko had tried to track down her daughter Kyoko, and the trail had led them to the United States. Although they did not find Kyoko and Tony, Yoko sued for custody of her daughter in Houston, and the court granted it on the condition that Yoko remain in the United States. She and John had then settled in Greenwich Village in New York City where they became friendly with radical political leaders like Jerry Rubin. At first John disliked and feared New York City, but he soon grew to love its stimulating atmosphere.

Influenced by their liberal friends, John and Yoko's songs on *Some Time in New York City* were very political. The cover of the LP bore the slogan "Ono News that's Fit to Print," a take-off on the *New York Times* motto, "All the news that's fit to print." And the sleeve itself looked like the layout of the paper as well.

Some Time in New York City was stark and unimaginative and the lyrics parroted the political clichés of the far left. It was very unpopular and even the liberal magazine *Rolling Stone* reviewed it unfavorably.

The radical tone of John's politics, however, brought him to the attention of John Mitchell, the U.S. Attorney General. When John's visa came up for renewal at the end of February, 1972, Mitchell pressured the U.S. Department of Immigration to refuse to renew it. Normally renewal was a routine process so the Department of Immigration cited his conviction for possession of marijuana as the reason for its refusal. Ordered to leave the United States, John lodged an appeal in court, and his case became a *cause célèbre.* Celebrities like

Dick Cavett rushed forward to testify as character references and thousands of people wore buttons proclaiming, "Let them stay."

His case dragged on for months and during this time, government officials had him followed and had his phone tapped. In search of privacy and greater security, John and Yoko moved from their brownstone townhouse into the Dakota. As always, though, the events of his life affected John's songwriting, and in his album *Mind Games* he included a fact sheet for an imaginary place called Nutopia, a country without boundaries or visas or passports. Two minutes of silence on the LP were devoted to the Nutopian national anthem.

John was struggling to keep working when his life hit a new low. Yoko threw him out because she needed "space to think." She resented losing her own identity, and she resented being in the spotlight constantly because she was John Lennon's wife. She wanted to find herself again, much as John had wanted to do when he was a Beatle.

John went to Los Angeles with his secretary May Pang, and for over a year he spent most of his time drinking and making headlines with his dissipated escapades and he called Yoko every week to ask whether he could return home. "Not yet," she continued to tell him, but she urged him to take care of himself. She never criticized him for his wild behavior; instead she told him that some of his antics were good "events."

While he was in Los Angeles, John attempted to produce an album of classic rock songs, but his producer Phil Spector disappeared with the tapes. John continued to drink until he finally realized he was falling deeper and deeper into a pit and pulled himself together. He stopped drinking, returned to New York, got an apartment, and plunged back into his work.

Although its tone was melancholy, his next album, *Walls and Bridges*, was far better than *Some Time in New York City* and *Mind Games*. Several songs were directed at Yoko but one bitter song, "Steel and Glass," was directed at Allan Klein. When Klein's contract with John, George, and Ringo expired in 1973, they had not renewed it, and Klein sued them for over twenty-two million dollars. The most popular song on *Walls and Bridges* was "Whatever Gets You Through the Night," which John had recorded with Elton John and released as a single. He promised to sing it with Elton in concert if it made the top of the charts. To John's surprise, the record did make number one, and he honored his promise. On November 28, 1974, John sang "Whatever Gets You Through the Night" at Elton's concert in Madison Square Garden.

Yoko was in the audience that night and after his performance, she went backstage to talk to John. Beginning that evening, John and Yoko dated until February when he quietly moved back into their apartment at the Dakota. He later told reporters, "The separation didn't work out." They made their first public appearance together at the Grammy Awards early in 1975.

John now turned back to the project he had started and abandoned in Los Angeles—an album of oldies but goodies, which he jokingly called "moldies but oldies." It contained his own favorite rock songs like "Be-Bop-a-Lula," "Stand By Me," "Do You Want to Dance" and "Sweet Little Sixteen," and it was a tremendous hit.

John's personal and professional lives were coming back together and he reached a zenith when Yoko became pregnant. They had longed for a child of their own since her miscarriage in 1968. John stopped working to care for Yoko during her pregnancy, but she was confined to the hospital for the last month. At one point she was given a blood transfusion with the wrong type blood. Yoko became rigid, and John yelled for help. When the doctor arrived, he went over to John and said, "I've always wanted to meet you." John was outraged. "My wife is dying and you want to talk about music," he cried. Once again he felt betrayed by fame. Fortunately, Yoko recovered, and she gave birth to their healthy son, Sean, on October 9, 1975. It was John's 35th birthday. Yoko was 43. Two days before his son was born, the U.S. Court of Appeals overturned the order to deport John.

Later in the month, John and Yoko released the LP *Shaved Fish*, a collection of the Plastic Ono Band's "greatest hits." On the cover was the line, "A conspiracy of silence speaks louder than words." It was attributed to Dr. Winston O'Boogie, John's favorite pseudonym. The public soon learned the meaning of the line, for John and Yoko stopped recording and withdrew from public life. They lived quietly, shunning discos and rock concerts. Occasionally, they attended classical music concerts or went out to dinner. They spent most of their time in their exquisitely furnished home.

John was afraid of burning out, rewriting old songs and singing all his greatest hits over and over again like Elvis. He wanted to free himself from his past and from fame and the obligations it carried. He later told *Newsweek* reporters, "The reason I became an artist was freedom, because I couldn't fit into the classroom, the college, the society. And that freedom was what I cherished—that was the plus for all the minuses of being an oddball." So John freed himself of his role as a rock star.

For five years John took over the role of housekeeper. He baked bread, washed and fed and diapered Sean, and ran the household. He was a totally different father to Sean than he was to Julian whom he rarely saw because he was often on tour. Julian grew up without knowing his father well. When Julian was small, John was a macho rock star. When Sean was born, John became a househusband and he was proud of his role. He described it as an "enlightening experience for me because it was a complete reversal of my upbringing. It's the wave of the future and I'm glad to be in the forefront. . . ."

Once John described himself as a combination of a "monk" and a "performing flea." The monk side dominated his life from 1975-79. He read books and magazines on everything from astrology to science and he re-read books about the life of Christ. He enjoyed studying ancient history and he liked to meditate in his isolation tank, a box-like enclosure that cuts out light and sound. Artist Roy Doremus, who painted murals of clouds in the Lennons' hall and bathroom, often saw John's footprints in the plush carpet leading to the tank.

Yoko, on the other hand, took over the responsibilities of their financial affairs, buying and selling real estate, managing their record deals, collecting Egyptian art, and raising dairy cows. Under her management their personal worth increased to over $150 million and they contributed 10 percent of their annual earnings to charity through their Spirit Foundation. They often gave to special causes such as the police officers' fund for bullet-proof vests or to drug rehabilitation programs; John, however, refused to give benefit performances, believing he had given enough of them in his career. He and Yoko personally packed food baskets for the poor every Thanksgiving and signed the cards tucked inside.

Although a handful of fans were usually on hand to greet him at the Dakota, the press forgot about John and Yoko and they lived like private citizens, not celebrities. Then as suddenly as they had disappeared, they re-emerged, placing an open letter in the Sunday papers in New York, London, and

John and Yoko arrive at the recording studio in New York to begin work on Double Fantasy *in August 1980.*

Tokyo on May 27, 1979. They described their last five years in seclusion as a time to "spring clean" their minds and to think about their future. They said that the world is facing hard times, but that they were optimistic about the future.

The next year they put their thought into the songs on *Double Fantasy*, their first album in five years. It included "Watching the Wheels," "Hard Times Are Over (for a while)," "One World, One People," and "Beautiful Boy," a song written for Sean. John told the press that he was rejuvenated and that his spirit "moved me to write suddenly, which I haven't done for a long, long time." In addition, John felt he had given Sean five years of his life and had established his goal of providing Sean with a loving and stable beginning in life. As always, John and Yoko's album was very autobiographical and "Starting Over" captured John's new mood. He was eager to begin a new chapter in his life. It was time for a change, time for a career again.

John was eagerly looking forward to the eighties for he had finally found the peace and contentment he had looked for his entire life. John Lennon's last message to the new generation was simple: Make your own dream come true. But he was unable to make his dream a reality. Shot and killed at the age of forty, he was unable to live out his fantasy: growing old with Yoko and laughing as they looked at their scrapbooks filled with articles and photographs about their antics, adventures, and contributions. But Yoko courageously said, " 'Starting Over' still goes. The '80s are still going to be a beautiful time and John believed in it . . . We had talked about living until we were eighty. We even drew up lists of all the things we could do together. Then it was all over. But that doesn't mean the message is over. The music will live on."

John's techniques were imitated by composers like Burt Bacharach, and his music influenced Bob Dylan, the Rolling Stones and many rock stars who followed him. His songs were recorded by countless singers from Frank Sinatra to Ella

Fitzgerald, from David Bowie and the Rolling Stones to avant-garde singer Cathy Berberian and blues singer Ray Charles. Even the Boston Pops Orchestra, led by Arthur Fiedler, recorded *Sgt. Pepper's Lonely Hearts Club Band.*

Singer Willie Nile said John put "honesty" and "truth" in rock and made all subjects the subjects of songs. Millions were cheered by his music and saw their lives mirrored in his work. Theater critic Clive Barnes wrote, "His voice in its time was the voice of youth all over the world. It was the voice of freedom over the chasms of generation gaps." John Lennon's songs changed the world of music and during the sixties, the world of music helped to change the world.

CHRONOLOGY

1940   John Lennon is born, October 9, in Liverpool, England.

1944   John goes to live with his Aunt Mimi and Uncle George in the Liverpool suburb of Woolton.

1945   John enters Dovedale Primary School.

1952   By now a reluctant student, John begins classes at Quarry Bank Grammar School.

1955   John adopts the "Ted" look and discovers rock 'n' roll.

           John loses a friend when his Uncle George dies suddenly.

1956   John gets his first guitar.

John organizes his own band, the Quarrymen, who play the popular "skiffle" music.

1957　John is introduced to Paul McCartney on June 15.

John enrolls at the Art College of Liverpool.

Later in the year he meets George Harrison.

1958　Julia Lennon is killed by a hit-and-run driver.

John begins to date Cynthia Powell, a fellow art student.

1960　After playing under a variety of names, John's group becomes the Beatles.

The Beatles are chosen to tour Scotland as backup group for the singer Johnny Gentle.

The Beatles are hired to play a club in Hamburg, Germany, and leave in August for a seventeen-week engagement.

1961　The group returns to Hamburg to play in another club.

While in Germany, the Beatles make their first recording as backup group for the British singer, Tony Sheridan, on the German Polydor label.

In the summer, the Beatles return to Liverpool and play in local clubs. Their popularity grows and the Beatles are voted the favorite group by readers of *Mersey Beat* magazine.

On November 9, Brian Epstein hears the Beatles and begins to think about managing them. In December, John accepts Brian's offer to become the Beatles' manager.

1962   The Beatles have their first record audition on New Year's Day but fail to get a contract with the record company, Decca.

In the spring the group returns to Hamburg for the third time.

The Beatles audition for George Martin in the summer.

Ringo Starr is hired to replace Pete Best as drummer.

John marries Cynthia Powell in Liverpool on August 23.

The Beatles are offered a contract by George Martin and make their first record, "Love Me Do."

1963   The Beatles appear on British TV for the first time on the variety show, "Thank Your Lucky Stars."

John's son Julian is born.

In March, the Beatles' second record, "Please Please Me," reaches the number one position on British record charts.

Beatlemania seizes Great Britain.

The Beatles appear at the Royal Command Performance at Buckingham Palace, though John is reluctant to accept the invitation.

1964   "I want To Hold Your Hand" hits number 1 in the United States on January 21.

On February 9, the Beatles appear on "The Ed Sullivan Show," and America is instantly caught up in Beatlemania.

By April, following their first U.S. tour, the Beatles have the top five songs on U.S. charts.

John publishes a book, *In His Own Write*, which helps establish his identity as an individual separate from the Beatles.

The Beatles' first movie, *A Hard Day's Night*, is released.

1965   The Beatles make a second successful tour of the U.S.

The movie *Help* is released, but John is not happy with the group's second attempt at filmmaking.

The album *Rubber Soul* is released, marking the beginning of the Beatles' experimentation with unusual instruments. This was also the first album whose cover the group designed themselves.

The Beatles are honored with Membership in the Order of the British Empire (MBE) for their services to British exports.

1966   The Beatles tour the U.S. for the third and last time.

John is criticized for his comments on religion but he is bewildered by the incident.

John accepts a role in the movie, *How I Won the War*, and goes to Spain for the filming.

With the album *Revolver*, the Beatles abandon what had become their characteristic sound in favor of songs that reflect the individuality of the group's members.

John meets artist Yoko Ono, and the two form a close friendship.

1967   The Beatles are voted the "most popular non-ideological idols" in a *Newsweek* magazine poll of college students.

Sgt. Pepper's Lonely Hearts Club Band is released to rave reviews. New York's *Village Voice* newspaper called it the "most successful record album ever issued."

In August, the Beatles meet Maharishi Mahesh Yogi at a transcendental meditation workshop in Wales and adopt the practice of TM.

Brian Epstein dies of an overdose of sleeping pills. John is particularly affected by the loss of the group's manager and his friend.

Apple Corps, Ltd. is formed to handle the Beatles' productions and business affairs.

The album *Magical Mystery Tour* is released, and the BBC television show on which it was based is panned by critics.

1968   John and Cynthia go to India with the other Beatles to study TM with the Maharishi.

On their return from India, John and Cynthia separate and eventually are divorced.

In July, John exhibits his artwork in an "all white" show in London. At the opening, he announces he will marry Yoko Ono.

The Beatles and *Abbey Road* are released and sell well, while John's records with Yoko are generally criticized and ridiculed by press and fans alike.

John and Yoko begin their peace campaign.

1969   John and Yoko are married in Gibraltor on March 20 and hold a "bed-in" for peace at the Hilton Hotel in Amsterdam, Holland.

John is named "Man of the Year" by *Rolling Stone* magazine.

In protest against the Vietnam War, John returns his MBE medal.

John tells the other Beatles he wants to leave the group.

1970   The Beatles break up officially, just before the release of their last movie, *Let It Be*, and the album of the same name.

1971	John begins primal therapy in Los Angeles at the Primal Institute.
	John records the album *Imagine*, whose title song is considered one of his best in the post-Beatle years.
1972	John fights a deportation order from the U.S. Department of Immigration when his visa is not renewed.
	John and Yoko separate and he moves to Los Angeles for a year.
1973	John returns to New York and continues to work, writing songs.
1974	John appears in concert with Elton John to sing their hit song, "Whatever Gets You Through the Night."
1975	John and Yoko are reconciled, and he moves back into their apartment at the Dakota.
	Son, Sean, is born to John and Yoko on October 9.
	A U.S. Court of Appeals overturns the deportation order that has been tied up in the courts since 1972.
	John withdraws from public life.
1975–79	John takes over management of the Lennon household, while Yoko assumes responsibility for their financial affairs.

1979   John and Yoko place open letters in newspapers in New York, London, and Tokyo describing their five years in seclusion and saying that they are looking toward the future.

John begins writing songs once again.

1980   The album *Double Fantasy* is released, John's first album in five years. The music indicates a new mood and a new chapter in his career.

John Lennon is assassinated in New York City on December 8.

FOR FURTHER READING

Aldridge, Alan (ed.). *The Beatles Illustrated Lyrics, Vol. 1.* New York: Delta/Seymour Lawrence, 1969.

_____ *The Beatles Illustrated Lyrics, Vol. 2.* New York: Delta/Seymour Lawrence, 1971.

The Beatles: The Fabulous Story of John, Paul, George and Ringo. London, Octopus Books Ltd., 1975.

Carr, Roy and Tony Tyler. *The Beatles: An Illustrated Record.* New York: Harmony Books, 1975.

Davies, Hunter. *The Beatles.* New York: McGraw-Hill Book Company, 1978.

Epstein, Brian. *A Cellarful of Noise.* New York: Doubleday and Company, 1964.

Fawcett, Anthony. *John Lennon: One Day at a Time.* New York: Grove Press, 1976.

Garbarini, Vic and Brian Cullman with Barbara Graustark. *Strawberry Fields Forever: John Lennon Remembered.* New York: Bantam Books, Inc., 1980.

Lennon, Cynthia. *A Twist of Lennon.* New York: Avon Books, 1978.

Lennon, John. *John Lennon, In His Own Write.* New York: Simon and Schuster, 1964.

_____ *A Spaniard in the Works.* New York: Simon and Schuster, 1965.

Norman, Philip. *Shout! The Beatles in Their Generation.* New York: Simon and Schuster, 1981.

Schaffner, Nicholas. *The Beatles Forever.* Harrisburg, Pa.: Cameron House, 1977.

Schaumburg, Ron. *Growing Up with the Beatles.* New York: Pyramid Books, 1976.

Swenson, John. *The John Lennon Story.* New York: Leisure Books, 1971.

INDEX

*Italicized page numbers
indicate photographs.*

10591

B Corbin, Carole Lynn
LEN
John Lennon

$11.90

DATE			

BIG HOLLOW SCHOOL
4499 N. HIGHWAY 2
INGLESIDE, ILLINOIS 60041